Study Guide with Text

to

Selected Poems
of
Robert Frost
1913-1923

by Ray Moore

Robert Frost between 1910 and 1920.

(Source: New York World-Telegram and the Sun Newspaper Photograph Collection, Library of Congress. There are no known restrictions on the usage of this photograph.)

Contents

Preface

A study guide is an *aid* to the close reading of a text, *never* a substitute for reading the text itself. This study guide aims to help readers/students come up with their own interpretations of Frost's poems, not to provide ready-made interpretations to be accepted uncritically and absorbed.

These poems deserve to be read *reflectively*, and the aim of this guide is to facilitate such a reading. The Guiding Questions have *no* answers provided. This is a deliberate choice. The questions are for readers who want to come to *their own conclusions* and not simply to be told what to think about it by someone else. Even 'suggested' answers would limit the *exploration of these texts* by readers which is the primary aim of the guide.

In the classroom, I found that students frequently came up with answers that I had not even considered, and, not infrequently, that they expressed their ideas better than I could have done. Teachers do not need their own set of predetermined answers in order effectively to evaluate the responses of their students.

Acknowledgements

As always, I am indebted to the work of numerous reviewers and critics. Where I am conscious of having taken an idea or a phrase from a particular author, I have cited the source in the text and the bibliography. Any failure to do so is an omission which I will immediately correct if it is drawn to my attention.

Literary works published in 1923 entered the public domain on January 1st, 2019, and more works will lose copyright protection each subsequent year. On this basis, all of the poems reproduced in this book are free from copyright. In addition, I believe that all quotations used in the analytical portions of my text fall under the definition of 'fair use.' If I am in error on any quotation, I will immediately correct it.

Thanks are due to my wife, Barbara, for reading the manuscript, for offering valuable suggestions, and for putting the text into the correct formats for publication. Any errors which remain are my own.

A Note on Pronouns

Frost was a man who tended to write about men. Given the age in which he wrote, that is not something for which he should be criticized. Thus, when he does not identify the gender of a speaker or character in his poems, we can generally assume that he intended the speaker or character to be male. Of course, it is perfectly possible for the reader to think of many of his unidentified speakers and characters as female. For example, "The Exposed Nest" works perfectly well if we assume that the speaker is female and the person being addressed is her daughter.

I have, however, stuck to the pronoun "he" in writing of Frost's unidentified speakers and characters. The use of 'he/she' gets clunky after a while, and the use of 'she' would be perverse.

Layout of the Text

The text of the poems and the questions is arranged so as to give maximum white space for readers who like to write their own reflections and notes.

In the first edition of *A Boy's Will* Frost added to the title of each poem an explanatory statement. These are not often included in editions of the poems but they are included here. "Reluctance" is one of the few exceptions.

Pre-reading Questions:

It is never a good idea to read a poem (or a novel, play or essay for that matter) without having some idea what it is about. For one thing, that is a very inefficient and time-wasting way to read. The pre-reading questions aim to get you thinking about the central ideas and experiences of each poem. If you are tempted to skip over this period of self-reflection and/or discussion, let me urge you not to do so – you will be cheating yourself. It would be rather like running the 100 meters without doing a warm-up – you will not run your best race and might end up injured! Group discussion if the best way to explore these questions, but a private reading journal is good too.

Study Guide Questions:

The questions are designed to help you to understand what each poem is about (its setting, characters, plot, themes, etc.) and how each poem is written (its verse structure, use of rhyme, imagery, symbolism, etc.). The full meaning of a poem can only be fully appreciated when both *what* the poem says and *how* the poem says it are seen in combination. Another way of saying this is that the style of a poem makes an essential contribution to the reader's experience of the meaning of the poem.

These questions do not normally have simple answers, nor is there always one answer. Consider a range of possible interpretations, preferably by discussing the questions with others. Disagreement is to be encouraged! However, if you are reading Frost's poems on your own you should consider keeping a reading journal in which you jot down your unfiltered reactions to each question, even if these are contradictory and confused. Such jottings will prove to be invaluable as a source when you decide that you are ready to firm up your response to each poem.

Final Thoughts

In this section I try to draw the strands of the poem together in some sort of conclusion. These commentaries do not claim to be either definitive or comprehensive. They represent my best understanding of each poem at this point in time.

Introduction to the Poetry of Robert Frost

The Issue of Interpretation

Michael Little writes of "Birches" that part of the appeal of the poem, "comes from the number of ideas it invites us to think about, all the while carefully avoiding telling us exactly what to think or what Frost wants us precisely to conclude about them" (152). Expanding on this theme, he writes of "Stopping by Woods on a Snowy Evening" that "The achievement of the poem is that it accommodates so many interpretative possibilities without forcing or excluding any of them" (189). The same might be said of most of Frost's poems (and certainly of the ones included here). On a first reading they are accessible: the language is that of normal speech and the situations they explore are ones with which readers can easily identify. Only on subsequent readings do the poems reveal depths of ambiguity and complexity which readers are left to understand and resolve in their own way.

Not everyone sees this as a strength. In his dissenting essay "Robert Frost: or, the Spiritual Drifter" (1948), Ivor Winters attacks Frost for writing in the voice of a plain-spoken countryman and thus for lacking the intellectual gravitas that Winters thinks essential to great poetry. He writes of "The Road Not Taken":

> [A] spiritual drifter is unlikely to have either the intelligence or the energy to become a major poet. Yet the poem has definite virtues, and these should not be overlooked. In the first place, spiritual drifters exist, they are real; and although their decisions may not be comprehensible, their predicament is comprehensible. The poem renders the experience of such a person, and renders the uncertain melancholy of his plight. Had Frost been a more intelligent man, he might have seen that the plight of the spiritual drifter was not inevitable, he might have judged it in the light of a more comprehensive wisdom.

Thus, for Winters, the great poet may *describe* people who lack moral compass or guidance, but may not himself *be* such a person. He continues, the "poem is good as far as it goes; the trouble is that it does not go far enough, it is incomplete, and puts on the reader a burden of critical intelligence which ought to be borne by the poet." Little and Winters are each pointing to the same characteristic in Frost's poetry; it is just that they

4

react differently to it.

It might be thought that Frost's own comments might give definitive insight into the intended meaning of his poems, since Frost wrote and spoke extensively on the subject of his own writing. Winters would have been just as disappointed with Frost as author as he was with his texts since Frost constantly refuses to explicate. Of "Stopping by Woods on a Snowy Evening" he said:

> That one I've been more bothered with more than anyone
> has ever been with any poem in just pressing it for more than
> it should be pressed for. It means enough without its being
> pressed. (Quoted in Fagan 318)

Arguing that the poem had been over-analyzed and over-interpreted, Frost concluded that the poem means "it's all very nice but I must be getting along, getting home" (Ibid.). Very few readers would accept that as a reading of "Stopping by Woods." Fortunately, authors do not have privileged control over how their texts are understood: readers will continue to find meanings texts that may or may not have been intended by their author. As readers, we are not required to prove that the writer intended a particular interpretation. Our sole responsibility is to show that a particular interpretation can be supported by the text rather than having been imposed upon the text.

Above all, Frost's poems encourage the reader to think for him/herself. Ivor Winter's may miss the presence of a towering genius using poetry to communicate great thought, but popular opinion does not.

Recurring Themes in Frost's Poetry

The subject matter (settings, incidents, plots, characters, etc.) of Frost's poems come from his own experience of farming in New England at the turn of the twentieth century. Frost wrote at a time when modernist poets were turning for their inspiration to what T. S. Eliot called the "Unreal city." Squires comments, "the typical modern poet has drawn his not from the City of God but from the city of man, from something that today is constantly failing" (4). In contrast, Frost stayed with the rural environment. The experiences recorded in his poems are those of farmers, their wives and farm laborers: cutting the grass and turning the hay; cleaning out winter debris from spring pools; picking apples at harvest time; a farmyard accident; etc. What is remarkable is that within this narrow, restricted canvas, Frost manages to explore universal themes and profound truths about the human condition. [I am reminded of Jane Austen's description of her own novels as, "the little bit (two inches wide) of ivory on which I work with so fine a brush, as produces so little effect after so much labour."]

The Natural World

> "I guess I'm not a nature poet, I have only written two poems
> without a human being in them" (Frost quoted in Fagan 394).

Robert Frost is not a nature poet: he is a poet of man's interaction with nature. To Frost, "nature is really an image of the whole world of circumstance within which man finds himself. It represents what one might call 'the human situation'" (Lynen, "Frost as Modern Poet" in Cox Ed. 177). There is nothing sentimental in the portrayal of nature in the poems. It is oftentimes beautiful and even inspiring, but just as often it is cold and life-threatening. Similarly, the people about whom Frost writes live in an uneasy relationship with nature. Some of them seem to live in harmony with the natural world, despite the fact that farming inevitably involves some adaptation of the natural environment to make it productive, but others exploit it destructively, stripping the land of trees and leaving it unproductive and open to erosion.

Montgomery writes that "From the publication of *A Boy's Will* ... Frost has indicated a realization that nature, *natura naturata*, not only will, but sometimes seems intended to, hurt those who love it ... Each man is, in a sense, a stranger in this world, and so he remains" ("Robert Frost and His Use of Barriers" in Cox Ed. 138, 148). Again and again, Frost makes the point that when people believe either that nature is on their side or that it is against them, they are making a grave error. In Frost's poems, flora and fauna are always indifferent to man. He seems to be saying that when people understand this, they will come to understand themselves better.

Ambiguity

> Frost believed that the surface of a poem, like speech, should be simple and immediate, yet that, upon further scrutiny, the poem should reveal itself as elusive. After all, life does not readily yield up its meaning and purpose – indeed, if it has any. The poet must be accurate in describing his limited sense of the mysteries of nature and of God, and he must be true to his own 'confusion' – to use one of Frost's favorite words. (Pack, "Frost's Enigmatic Reserve…" in Bloom ed. 9)

A man going home through the snow in a horse-drawn sled stops for a few minutes to look into a beautiful wood, then resumes his journey home. What could be simpler? But: Who is the man? Where has he come from? Why is he so drawn to the wood? What might the wood symbolize? What is the significance of his decision to return home? He says he has "miles to go" before he sleeps. What does that mean? "Stopping by Woods" is typical of Frost's poems in that it opens possibilities of interpretation that the poet seems deliberately to leave open. Ambiguity seems to Frost to be an essential element of the human condition. Frost wrote that what he valued most in poetry was "the pleasure of ulteriority" which he defined as "saying one thing and meaning another, saying one thing in terms of another" (quoted in Kendall 3).

Isolation and Communication

> [Frost's poetry is characterized] by the representation of the terrible actualities of life in a new way. I think of Frost as a terrifying poet … The universe he conceives is a terrible universe … [W]henever have people been so isolated, so lightening-blasted, so tried down and calcined by life, so reduced, each in his own way, to some last irreducible core of being … The manifest America of Mr. Frost's poems may be pastoral; the actual America is tragic. (Trilling, "A Speech on Frost" in Cox ed. 156-157)

The critic Lionel Trilling said this in a speech at a dinner celebrating Robert Frost's eighty-fifth birthday, at the Waldorf-Astoria Hotel in the spring of 1959. Trilling did not mean his remarks to be controversial, nor did he mean them to be negatively critical: he thought he was praising Frost. However, those readers who had come to see Frost as a genial, reassuring, avuncular, wise old farmer were shocked by Trilling's assertion that he was, on the contrary, a "terrifying poet."

In the years since Trilling's speech, and the critical fire-storm that it ignited, his view appears to have won the day. Thus, Lynen writes:

> Frost does not depict the outward events and conditions, but the central facts of twentieth century experience, the uncertainty and the painful sense of loss, are there and seem if anything more bleakly apparent in that their social and economic manifestations have been stripped away ... The question is not whether Frost depicts the scenery of modern life, but whether he deals with its major problems. (Lynen "Frost as Modern Poet" in Cox Ed. 190)

The people in Frost's poems live isolated lives. They do not generally live even in the small New England towns but in farmhouses widely spread through the countryside, frequently occupied by only a man and his wife, and often on a temporary basis to judge from the number of abandoned farms and shacks in the poems. Their loneliness is not, however, simply a geographical and historical accident; it is presented as an essential part of the human condition. The men tend to work on their own, but at least they have manual labor to occupy them. This gives them something to pass their time and a product in which they can take pride – a re-built wall, a well-mown field, a cleared spring, etc. With so much less to do, the women suffer far more from isolation, even to the point of psychosis.

Frost "knows that if alienation could be overcome by the repeated affirmation of fellowship, it would have disappeared a long time ago" (O'Donnell "Robert Frost and New England..." in Cox Ed 52). Nevertheless, every opportunity for friendly interaction is welcomed (repairing a dry-stone wall together, going over to talk to a passing neighbor), but again these activities are generally male. The women feel the lack of community much more deeply than do their menfolk who are frequently insensitive to how the women feel.

Barriers

To Frost, barriers between man and man "serve as a framework for mutual understanding and respect. It is because of barriers that we understand each other, and, far from striving to tear them down as is the modern tendency, Frost insists on recognizing them" (Montgomery, "Robert Frost and His Use of Barriers" in Cox Ed. 147). Readers who tend to assume that Frost sympathizes with the anti-wall sentiments of the narrator in "Mending Wall" are surprised that his poems consistently point to the importance of traditional barriers between people. Individual needs their own space. Paradoxically, that is a precondition of friendship, community and cooperation.

The role of fate and chance

To be versed in "Country Things" is at accept the role played in life by happenstance. Those who live in the country learn from experience that nature is indifferent to human affairs and that humans are in a vulnerable position – a life can be snuffed out by a sudden accident; a farm can cease to be viable as a result of a poor harvest; a marriage can be effectively ended by the death of a child. Even a cursory look at Frost's own life shows that he knew his share of sorrow.

The SparkNotes editors point out that "Nature poets tend to be deists, they discerned the existence of a benign creator in the beauties of the natural world – just as in looking at a watch we sense the existence of a watchmaker. Frost never had this transcendental experience. In Frost's world, God is either absent or indifferent to the plight of humans who are victims of fate or chance." The people in Frost's poems tend not to sentimentalize tragedies or to reach out to religion for consolation: like the farmworkers who witness the death of a child in "'Out, Out —'" they turn to "to their affairs" because they "[w]ere not the one dead," and with a realism that shocks many readers, they accept that the boy's death "ended it" leaving "[n]o more to build on there." One senses that Frost understands and even sympathizes with such realism.

Time and Mortality

Individuals (whether we are speaking of humanity, fauna or flora) are subject to linear time: time destroys the beauty of people, animals and flowers. As Squires puts it, "Change is the presumed necessity of nature … only change is permanent … The grand pattern of decline and renewal, birth and death, summer and winter comes to represent an eternity or permanence " (38-40). However, Frost is also aware that in the wider context of nature, time is cyclical: the family goes on; animals give birth and rear their young; and dead winter gives was to budding spring. There is some consolation in this dual perspective.

The Role of Poetry

The protagonist-narrators in Frost's poems are often unsatisfied with their existence in the real world in which others of his characters seem to live quite contentedly. Frost's speakers are often aware of two worlds: the rational world of scientific truth and the imaginative world of creative truth. Only the latter appears to offer insight into the true nature of human existence in the world. In intense moments of contemplation can a person achieve a higher, spiritual consciousness. In the poems, this is always described in symbols (climbing an elm tree, climbing a ladder up to pick apples, going into the dark woods, etc.), but it is clear that for Frost the reading and writing of poetry was one way to achieve this imaginative truth. It is, however, a state that cannot be sustained for long. The climber of elms and of apple trees much come back down to earth, and the gazer into the dark woods must return to the real world of duties, obligations and tasks to be completed. What poetry does (like the well-made wood-pile or a clump of flowers deliberately left uncut by a mower) is to provide evidence of the journey.

Stylistic Features of Frost's Poetry

> Robert Frost's elegant poetry stands alone. It is "modern"
> only in the sense that it is not Victorian or Georgian … But
> Frost's poetry is not modern in the sense that it is like any
> other poetry of the twentieth century. Not even in the matter
> of superficial form: diction, trope, technical versification …
> The whole form of Frost's knowledge is different from that
> of the typical contemporary. (Squires 1-3)

Frost wrote at a time when many poets were abandoning traditional verse forms in favor of more experimental poetry. T. S. Eliot, a fellow American who had also come to England to pursue his writing career, led the way with his use of free-verse (i.e., verse without any set rhyme or rhythm) in poems such as "The Love Song of J. Alfred Prufrock" (1915) and "The Waste Land" (1922). Frost compared the composition of free-verse poetry to playing tennis without a net up: it might be fun, but it "ain't tennis." Frost enjoyed the discipline and restrictions of the net.

Language

> Mr. Frost's people are distinctly real. Their speech is real; he
> has known them. I don't want much to meet them, but I know
> that they exist, and what is more, that they exist as he has

portrayed them. (Ezra Pound)

Pound was one of the first critics to note that Frost made a conscious effort to use of colloquial language rather than the heightened language usually associated with poetry. His decision to do so certainly makes his poetry accessible to a wider audience and is one of the main reasons for his popularity at a time when poetry was becoming distinctly a minority genre. Frost's greatest skill was to constrain colloquial diction and rhythms within formal poetic structures yet still produce poems that seem to embody natural and spontaneous speech.

Verse Form and Rhyme

Kendall makes the important point that Frost, "considered that measure gave the poet freedom within bounds (which was the only meaningful freedom), and insisted that only two meters were permitted – 'strict iambic and loose iambic' ... [adding that] a line might be any length up to sex feet" (9). Thus, he used a wide variety of traditional verse forms, including the sonnet (for which he had a particular fondness), the dramatic monologue, the narrative and the lyric. Free verse (unrhymed, irregular verse) he rejected. Frost generally writes in iambic meter (feet composed of stressed/unstressed syllables) whether he wrote rhymed or unrhymed verse. He often uses blank (i.e., unrhymed) verse, that is, iambic pentameter (five iambic feet in each line).

First-person narrative

Frost frequently uses a first-person narrator as the voice of a poem. This allows the reader insight into the speaker's life at a significant moment and creates an impression of reliability because we tend to trust what the sympathetic narrator tells us. However, readers need to proceed with caution. It is far too easy to assume that the voice we hear is that of the poet himself or that the poet automatically endorses the speaker's viewpoint. Remember that the first person narrator is an imagined character in the poem in the way that a third person narrator is not. (The same is obviously true of novels. *Lolita* [1955] is narrated by Humbert Humbert, a completely unreliable, self-delusional pedophile and murderer, a fictional character invented by the author Vladimir Nabokov.) With each poem we have to ask whether Frost intends his first-person narrator to be reliable or unreliable. It is probably best to be skeptical. Even if we conclude that the narrator of a particular poem is presented as reliable, we should still be cautious in simply identifying the narrator with the poet. At best, a first-person narrator can only be a simplified, fictionalized version of the complex human being who wrote the poem.

Narrative

A story, or an incident, is at the heart of most of Frost's poems. The poet presents a series of events and actions, normally through the eyes of a narrator, which lead to a climax and resolution.

A Boy's Will (1913)

Introduction

Literary works cannot be 'explained' by reference to the author's biography. Nevertheless, knowing something about the life of a writer can add to a reader's understanding and appreciation of his/her writing. Deirdre Fagan quotes Frost as having written that the poems in *A Boy's Will* were "pretty near being the story of five years" (*Critical Companion to Robert Frost,* 52). The poems in that collection had been written over the previous two decades.

Robert Lee Frost (March 26th, 1874 – January 29th, 1963) published his first poem in the magazine of Lawrence High School from where he graduated in 1892. Two years later, the *New York Independent* paid him $15.00 for "My Butterfly." In 1894, Frost paid for the publication of two copies of his poems (one for himself and one for Elinor White, his high school sweetheart). Frost attended both Dartmouth College (for two months) and Harvard University (for two years, 1897 – 1899), but left both without graduating. On December 19th, 1895, he married Elinor, who had refused his earlier proposals because she wanted to finish college before marrying. Their first child, Eliot, was born the following year. From his grandfather, Frost inherited a farm near Derry, New Hampshire, on condition that he farm it for at least ten years, and here he worked supporting his wife and four young children while also writing poetry. Failing to make a success of farming, Frost taught English at Pinkerton Academy, New Hampshire (1906-1911) and the New Hampshire Normal School (later Plymouth State University) in Plymouth.

By 1911, Frost was free to sell the Derry farm and having failed to find a publisher for his growing body of poetry in the United States he decided to take his family to England to pursue his literary career there. In August, 1912, the Frost family sailed from Boston to Glasgow on the USS *Parisian* and found a house in Beaconsfield, a small town outside of London. *A Boy's Will* (1913) was published by the firm of the late David Nutt having been accepted by Nutt's widow, though the terms of publication were not generous. Frost, who was now 38, became actively involved in London literary circles where he met the American poet Ezra Pound (1885 – 1972) who wrote favorable reviews of *A Boy's Will* in the influential magazines *Poetry* and *The Smart Set.* The collection, Pound said, "has the tang of the New Hampshire woods, and it has just this utter sincerity. It is not post-

Miltonic or post-Swinburnian or post Kiplonian. This man has the good sense to speak naturally and to paint the thing, the thing as he sees it." Other positive reviews followed, and the collection was a success. Frost and Pound would soon part company because Frost felt that Pound, who was experimenting with new forms of 'modernist' poetry, was trying to change his own more traditional poetic style. Nevertheless, by that time Frost had made the acquaintance of poets such as Gibson, Lascelles Abercrombie, and W. H. Davies (collectively known as the Georgian poets).

The title of Frost's first collection comes from the repeated lines in the poem "My Lost Youth" (1874) by Henry Wadsworth Longfellow: "A boy's will is the wind's will / And the thoughts of youth are long, long thoughts." That line is, in turn, a quote from *Moarsi favrrot* (1675) by Olaus Matthiae Lappo-Sirma: "A boy's mood is the wind's mood, / the thoughts of youth are long thoughts."

Into My Own

The youth is persuaded that he will be rather more than less himself for having forsworn the world.

Pre-reading

1. Ever wanted to leave home? I mean, just up and walk away? What would you be escaping from? What would you be escaping to?
2. What are the things in your future that you find exciting and what are the things that worry you (going to college, entering a relationship, buying/renting a house, getting old, dying, etc.)? How confident do you feel in your ability to cope with your future?

ONE of my wishes is that those dark trees,
So old and firm they scarcely show the breeze,
Were not, as 'twere, the merest mask of gloom,
But stretched away unto the edge of doom.

I should not be withheld but that some day   5
Into their vastness I should steal away,
Fearless of ever finding open land,
Or highway where the slow wheel pours the sand.

I do not see why I should e'er turn back,
Or those should not set forth upon my track   10
To overtake me, who should miss me here
And long to know if still I held them dear.

They would not find me changed from him they knew—
Only more sure of all I thought was true.

A Boy's Will

Guiding Questions
First Quatrain (Lines 1-4):
1. What does the speaker mean when he calls the dark trees that he sees (perhaps from his window) "the merest mask of gloom"? (Clue: This is a metaphor. Think about a grotesque mask someone might wear at a fancy-dress party.) Comment on the effect of the alliteration used in this phrase.
2. He imagines the trees "stretched away unto the edge of doom." What have they come to represent (symbolize) in his imagination? (Frost borrows the phrase "edge of doom" from Sonnet 116 by William Shakespeare.)
Second Quatrain (Lines 5-8):
3. The phrase "that some day" is rather unusual. What does the poem gain by the use of "some"?
4. He says he wants to "steal away." From what is it that he wants to escape? What kinds of forces might try to withhold him, prevent him from walking away into the trees?
5. Look more closely at how lines 5 and 6 are written. Notice that line five has no end-stop punctuation, so it runs-on to line six (a technique called enjambment). Also notice the alliteration in "Should steal." What do these two stylistic features add to the feel of these lines?
6. What is it that he wants to find or experience? Having started his journey through the trees he has no fears of never finding "open land" (as a sailor might anticipate finding 'open sea.') What do you think that symbolizes? Alternatively, he has no fears of *not* finding the "highway where the slow wheel pours the sand." What do you think that symbolizes? (Remember that when this poem was written automobiles were relatively new and highways, particularly in rural areas, were often little more than sandy dirt roads.)
Third Quatrain (Lines 9-12):
7. What is your reaction to the speaker's statement that once he is gone, "I do not see why I should e'er turn back"? Is he right that there would be no reason for him ever to come back?
8. The speaker feels that others would follow and overtake him on his journey. Perhaps surprisingly, he expresses the hope that his loved ones *will* follow and find him when he is on his trek. Why does he want this to happen? (Clue: *One* of the things Frost is writing about in this poem is his writing. Writing poems is not much use if no one ever reads them.)
Final Couplet (Lines 13-14):
9. What do you think that the speaker means by the last two lines? He seems confident that his quest will not fundamentally have changed him. How do

16

you react to this confidence?

Holistic:

10. The poem is a sonnet. It is written in rhyming couplets arranged into three quatrains and a final couplet (AABB CCDD EEFF GG). Do you find any relationship between the division into verses and the stages of the speaker's developing thoughts? What effect is gained by having the speaker's final thought expressed in a couplet?

11. What have you learned about the identity of the speaker who provides the voice of the poem? Consider both the circumstances of his life (age, family, neighborhood, etc.) and his character/personality. (Note: The speaker is not simply Robert Frost.)

12. Explain the title of the poem. Specifically, what does the speaker mean by "My Own"?

13. What effect does the regularity of the form in this poem (particularly the rhyme scheme and the iambic pentameter meter of the lines) have on you?

Final Thoughts

Frost wrote of this poem in a letter dated January 21st, 1913, "When the life of the streets perplexed me a long time ago[,] I attempted to find an answer to it for myself by going literally into the wilderness" (quoted in Fagan 181). The speaker in the poem wants to be his own person and choose his own way. He feels constricted by the range of experience he has lived to this point and the need to go beyond it. His aim is not, however, to get out into the big world (the world of "open land" and highways) and make his fortune. This is a world where "where the slow wheel pours the sand," a metaphor for the inevitable passage of time (as in sand running through an hourglass). The image captures human helplessness in the face of mortality. Rather the speaker wants to look inward, to confront the darkest aspects of human consciousness right up to "the edge of doom." Cowley writes that the woods are a symbol "for the uncharted country within ourselves, full of possible beauty, but also full of horror" ("The Case Against Mr. Frost" in Cox Ed.). The poem, then, is about a quest into human consciousness, a quest to understand the nature of human existence, rather than a real journey into the world. It is about a quest to deepen the understanding. The speaker is an artist who wants to explore the full implications of the human condition. That is why he is anxious for those he loves to follow him. His is not an individual quest undertaken only for his own edification; he sees himself as a leader whose journey will benefit others. The speaker's self-confidence in the final couplet seems a little naïve. A more mature approach to the sort of quest he envisages would include some awareness that it might change himself quite fundamentally. Is Frost aware of this shallow, self-assured arrogance in his narrator? Each reader must decide that for him/herself.

Storm Fear

He is afraid of his own isolation.

Pre-reading

Ever been in physical danger because of the weather? I mean like lightening, a hurricane, a tornado, etc. Explain the circumstances. What did it feel like?

When the wind works against us in the dark,
And pelts with snow
The lowest chamber window on the east,
And whispers with a sort of stifled bark,
The beast,   5
"Come out! Come out!" –
It costs no inward struggle not to go,
Ah, no!
I count our strength,
Two and a child,   10
Those of us not asleep subdued to mark
How the cold creeps as the fire dies at length, –
How drifts are piled,
Dooryard and road ungraded,
Till even the comforting barn grows far away   15
And my heart owns a doubt
Whether 'tis in us to arise with day
And save ourselves unaided.

Guiding Questions

Lines 1-10:

1. How does the poet in these lines make the wind appear threatening and convey the anxiety of the speaker? (Why do you think the poet specifies "the lowest chamber window"? What might it represent/symbolize? Consider the metaphor in lines 4-5 and the personification in line 6.)

2. Comment on the irony of the lines, "I count our strength, / Two and a child."

Lines 11-15:

3. What changes does the speaker note? How does the speaker's description of these changes increase the reader's feeling of the power of the storm and the potential threat to the "Two and a child"?

4. In lines 14-15, he is describing the way in which the normality of the landscape becomes erased as the blanketing snow gets deeper. How does the snow 'ungrade' the yard and road? How does it make the barn appear farther away?

Lines 16-18:

5. What is the "doubt" that enters the speaker's mind here?

6. How does the conclusion of this poem relate to the theme of a poem such as "The Tuft of Flowers"?

Holistic:

7. As you read through the poem what details did you get of the narrator's situation and the setting of the action?

8. The rhyme-scheme of the poem is patternless: ABCACDBBEFGEFHIJIH. The poet also makes use of some mid-line rhyme. What does the poet's flexible use of rhyme add to the experience of reading the poem?

9. The basic meter of the poem is iambic pentameter, but half-lines continually disrupt this pattern. Comment on the poet's use of half-lines.

10. The storm may, of course, simply be a storm. (The winters in New England can be brutal, as described in Edith Wharton's novella *Ethan Frome* [1911].). It might, however, be symbolic. Explore what kind of life-challenges the storm might represent.

10. The poem can be interpreted on three levels: the purely physical, the psychological, and the spiritual/religious. Explain each level of interpretations. How are they similar and how different?

11. Do you find this, on balance, an optimistic or a pessimistic poem?

Final Thoughts

Paul Simon (born 1941) sings, "I am a rock. I am an island," while John Donne (1572-1631) writes "No man is an island entire of itself; every man is a piece of the continent, a part of the main." In Simon's song, the speaker has been hurt in love and has chosen isolation as the best way to avoid further pain; in Donne's poem every man is inevitably "involved in mankind" and therefore isolation is not a realistic option.

Every reader of this poem will have encountered challenges that seemed insuperable, whether these threatened his/her physical or psychological well-being. The question this Frost poem raises is whether there are some challenges over which we cannot triumph alone. Perhaps we need the support of a community to help dig us out; perhaps we need faith in a god to keep us from becoming snowed under. Frost's poem poses the question and leaves it to the reader to ponder the answer. The fate of the snow-bound family is left hanging in the balance.

Mowing

He takes up life simply with the small tasks.

Pre-reading

Ever spent hours, even a whole day or days, alone while doing a demanding, repetitive physical task (something equivalent to cutting long grass with an old scythe)? What did you think about as you worked? Did the work fall into a rhythm? What was the point of your work? What did you personally get out of the experience?

There was never a sound beside the wood but one,
And that was my long scythe whispering to the ground.
What was it it whispered? I knew not well myself;
Perhaps it was something about the heat of the sun,
Something, perhaps, about the lack of sound —   5
And that was why it whispered and did not speak.
It was no dream of the gift of idle hours,
Or easy gold at the hand of fay or elf:
Anything more than the truth would have seemed too weak
To the earnest love that laid the swale in rows,   10
Not without feeble-pointed spikes of flowers
(Pale orchises), and scared a bright green snake.
The fact is the sweetest dream that labor knows.
My long scythe whispered and left the hay to make.

Notes:

A "fay" is a fairy or elf. A "swale" is the term used in New England for a low-lying, marshy meadow. "Orchises" are orchids (normally tropical flowers) that grow on the ground in temperate regions.

23

Guiding Questions

Lines 1-6:

1. The speaker is cutting grass to make hay for fodder by the side of a wood. He becomes fascinated by the swishing sound that his scythe makes and wonders about the significance of its "whispering" as though it were secretly trying to tell the ground something. (To state the obvious, the idea of the scythe "whispering" involves personification.) How does the sound of the words and their rhythm convey the swishing sound of the scythe cutting through the grass as it swings forward and then through the air as it swings back? (Examine in particular the effect of the oft-repeated letters 'w' and 's', and the inversion of the line-opening in lines 4 and 5: "Perhaps it was something ... Something, perhaps...")

Lines 7-12:

2. In lines 7-8 the speaker makes, and rejects, two suggestions as to what the scythe might be saying. What are they? Why does he reject these ideas?
3. What do you understand by the lines, "Anything more than the truth would have seemed too weak / To the earnest love that laid the swale in rows"? What is the "truth" that he has identified in the scythe's whispering?
4. The action of cutting the grass is constructive, for the grass will make hay. Nevertheless, it is also destructive. What two destructive features of grass cutting are mentioned?

Lines 13-14:

5. In the last two lines of the poem, what conclusion does the speaker draw about the meaning of the scythe's sound? What is the "fact" that the scythe whispered?

Holistic:

6. This is a sonnet with the following unusual irregular rhyme scheme: ABCABD ECDGEH GH. In terms of rhyme, it draws a little from both Petrarchan and Shakespearean forms. Like Petrarch's sonnets (which rhyme ABBAABBA CDECDE), the poem divides into an octet (the first eight lines) and a sextet (the last six lines) with a volta, or thematic turning point, in line 9. How is this division made clear by end of line punctuation? Describe the theme of the octet and the theme of the sextet. However, like Shakespeare's sonnets (which rhyme ABAB CDCD EFEF GG), the turning point and the impact of "Mowing" comes in its two final lines, although Shakespeare typically ends with a couplet which Frost does not do here. In what ways are the final two lines distinct from the rest of the poem poetically and/or thematically?

7. The meter is a variation on iambic pentameter. Each line has five stressed syllables separated by varying numbers of unstressed syllables (so the lines do not all have ten syllables). Only line 12 is strictly iambic. How does Frost exploit the freedom of meter that he gives himself?

8. Like many of Frost's poems, "Mowing" invites more symbolic interpretations. What do you think that the poem may be saying about life, work, sex, writing poems, art, etc?

9. Only when you have answered the question above, read this:

> As a statement about art in general and poetry in particular, the poem tells us that the Real, the common voice, the realities of work and labor - these are sweet; poetry inheres [i.e., exists essentially or permanently] in these things and need not be conjured through willful imagining, flights of fancy (elves), or an abandonment of the everyday. In fact, anything "more than the truth" is debilitating to art.
>
> As a statement about living, the poem seems to say that working in the world, embracing and engaging its facts through action, is a prerequisite for knowledge about it. Truth comes before understanding, and truth must be worked for. And so the challenge for the liver of life – and for the poem, and for the reader of poetry – is to work to embody that physical, factual, sensory truth.
>
> (SparkNotes Editors, "Frost's Early Poems")

Do these two paragraphs change your ideas? How?

Final Thoughts

The poem is a meditation by a mower on the significance of the sound his scythe makes as it slices through the grass in a field beside a wood. The first eight lines (the octet) describe the sound of the scythe and speculate on its meaning and significance. The last six lines (the sestet) reject any magical or spiritual interpretation of the sound, concluding that the sound is the product of labor, of the interaction of humans and nature – no greater explanation is either necessary or possible.

As so often a simple poem about mowing a field invites a more complex interpretation. The act of making hay may symbolize the act of making poetry. Both the mower and the poet put things in order, the mower by laying the "swale in rows" of grass and the poet by putting his ideas down in poetic form (in this case a sonnet). The rows are not mathematically precise, just as the lines of poetry in this sonnet do not precisely follow a specific sonnet form, but order has been brought in both cases, and perhaps that is the best we can hope to do in our lives. The 'meaning' of life lies in the sensuous joy we take in the pleasurable experience of work.

The Tuft of Flowers

about fellowship (sic)

Pre-reading:

Ever felt really alone? I mean, felt like you would never connect with another human being ever again? Describe how you felt.
Ever seen something made by another human being, something not made specifically for you at all, but to which you could relate; something perhaps made long ago that made it possible for you to really empathize with the person who made it?

I went to turn the grass once after one
Who mowed it in the dew before the sun.

The dew was gone that made his blade so keen
Before I came to view the levelled scene.

I looked for him behind an isle of trees;   5
I listened for his whetstone on the breeze.

But he had gone his way, the grass all mown,
And I must be, as he had been, – alone,

"As all must be," I said within my heart,
"Whether they work together or apart."   10

But as I said it, swift there passed me by
On noiseless wing a 'wildered butterfly,

Seeking with memories grown dim o'er night
Some resting flower of yesterday's delight.

And once I marked his flight go round and round,   15
As where some flower lay withering on the ground.

And then he flew as far as eye could see,
And then on tremulous wing came back to me.

I thought of questions that have no reply,
And would have turned to toss the grass to dry;   20

But he turned first, and led my eye to look
At a tall tuft of flowers beside a brook,

A leaping tongue of bloom the scythe had spared
Beside a reedy brook the scythe had bared.

I left my place to know them by their name,   25
Finding them butterfly weed when I came.

The mower in the dew had loved them thus,
By leaving them to flourish, not for us,

Nor yet to draw one thought of ours to him.
But from sheer morning gladness at the brim.   30

The butterfly and I had lit upon,
Nevertheless, a message from the dawn,

That made me hear the wakening birds around,
And hear his long scythe whispering to the ground,

And feel a spirit kindred to my own;   35
So that henceforth I worked no more alone;

But glad with him, I worked as with his aid,
And weary, sought at noon with him the shade;

And dreaming, as it were, held brotherly speech
With one whose thought I had not hoped to reach.   40

"Men work together," I told him from the heart,
"Whether they work together or apart."

Study Guide

Guiding Questions

Lines 1-10:

1. The poem describes two workers on the same farm, though in the course of the poem they never actually see each other. What is it that each is doing?

2. What does the speaker mean when he concludes that "'all must be [alone] … / Whether they work together or apart'"? What has led him to this thought?

Lines 11-24:

3. What in the description of the speaker's awareness of the butterfly suggests that it has been sent (in some mystical way) to lift his despair?

4. What has happened to the "resting flower" for which the butterfly is seeking? How does the butterfly react? In what way(s) is the butterfly as 'lost' as is the speaker? What do you think that the speaker means by the line, "I thought of questions that have no reply"? Suggest some of those questions.

5. What is the effect of the metaphor, "A leaping tongue of bloom" that the speaker uses to describe the spared flowers? (You might recall in *Exodus* God speaking to Moses from the middle of a burning bush or the reference in the *Book of the Acts of the Apostles* to the Holy Spirit descending on the disciples in tongues of flame some time after the crucifixion of Christ.) What message do the flowers communicate to the speaker?

Lines 25-30:

6. The speaker ponders the mower's motives for leaving the tuft of flowers uncut. What possible motives does he reject? How does he finally explain the mower's action? (Explore the metaphor, "sheer morning gladness at the brim." Clue: Think of a glass of wine [or cola] full to the top.)

Lines 31-42:

7. Comment on the two meanings of the highlighted words, "The butterfly and I had *lit upon* / …a message from the dawn." (Clue: Think back to the "leaping tongue of bloom" metaphor.)

8. Why does the speaker say that he has received "a message from the dawn"? (Remember that the first man was cutting the grass just after dawn to avoid the heat of the day.) What effect does the message have upon the speaker? How does it enable him to empathize with the unseen man?

Holistic:

9. Contrast the meaning of the lines: "'alone / As all must be,' I said within my heart," and, "'Men work together,' I told him from the heart."

10. The poem is written in twenty heroic couplets (i.e., rhyming couplets in

iambic pentameter), although Frost introduces some variation on the strict iambic foot (stressed/unstressed). All rhymes are full rhymes, and the majority of lines are end-stopped. How does this contribute to the effect of the poem when you read it?

11. Frost introduces a few archaic-sounding words such as "o'er night" and "henceforth". What is the effect of these words?

12. The "heart / apart" rhyme of lines 9-10 gets repeated in lines 41-42. Two additional end-words, "[a]round / alone / ground," are repeated on lines 8 and 15-16 and 33-34 and 36. What is the effect of this repetition?

13. Deirdre Fagan. quotes Frost as having written that "Into My Own" expressed how he turned away from people and "Tuft of Flowers" showed how he "came back to them" (*Critical Companion to Robert Frost*, 52). What light does this comment by the author throw on your understanding of this poem?

Final Thoughts

The profound sense of loneliness that the speaker experiences is more than the temporary loneliness of a morning spent working alone in a field seeing no other human being. It is the existential loneliness of the human condition. Not only is each person isolated from every other person, but it seems that man's relationship with nature is essentially a destructive one. The man who came before cutting the grass had a "blade so keen" that it 'levelled [the] scene." A returning butterfly (surely one of the most beautiful and fragile of nature's creatures) is bewildered because the scene that it vaguely remembers from the day before is utterly changed. The flower on which it landed yesterday lies "withering on the ground." In confusion, the butterfly goes around in circles and then comes back to the speaker as if asking for an explanation. T

he speaker, however, is all out of answers and can only think of returning to his mechanical task: he has reached his lowest point in the poem. However, nature, in the form of the butterfly, offers an answer of its own. The butterfly discovers a clump of flowers beside "a reedy brook," and the speaker immediately senses that its "leaping tongue of bloom" has a message for him. He instinctively understands that the mower left this clump of flowers standing because he "loved them thus." He did it not for the butterfly or for the man, but from simple, disinterested joy in the beauty of the flowers. Because he is capable of empathizing with the man, the speaker feels at one with him and with the natural world that surrounds them both, "glad with him, I worked as with his aid." The poem ends on a very positive note: people can exist in harmony with nature and that harmony is what unites them.

Now Close the Windows

It is time to make an end of speaking.

Pre-reading

Ever meditate? Ever want to just cut yourself off from external stimuli and reach down into the silence within? How do you do this? How does it make you feel?

NOW close the windows and hush all the fields;
  If the trees must, let them silently toss;
No bird is singing now, and if there is,
  Be it my loss.
It will be long ere the marshes resume,   5
  It will be long ere the earliest bird:
So close the windows and not hear the wind,
  But see all wind-stirred.

Guiding Questions

1. What do you learn of, or what do you imagine about, the setting of the poem (location, time of day, season of the year, etc.)?
2. In the first line, the speaker uses the imperative voice ("close … hush all the fields … let them …"). Is he addressing himself, another person in the house with him, or the reader?
3. Why would the speaker want to block out the sound of the world outside his window?

Final Thoughts

This is such a simple poem that it almost defies analysis – almost. The speaker wants some respite from the outside world which is represented by the wind that is tossing the branches of the trees. It is not as though there is a storm outside, just a strong wind, but that wind represents a world in continuous motion. What the speaker wants is some a sort of time-out, a space of a few hours to regroup before having to venture again into the real world in which he must live. That call will come from the marsh birds in the morning, and having taken some time to himself, he will be ready for it.

October

He sees days slipping from him that were the best for what they were.

Pre-reading

How do you feel about getting old? What age do you consider old? Why?
How will your life be different when you are that age?

O HUSHED October morning mild,
Thy leaves have ripened to the fall;
To-morrow's wind, if it be wild,
Should waste them all.
The crows above the forest call;   5
To-morrow they may form and go.
O hushed October morning mild,
Begin the hours of this day slow,
Make the day seem to us less brief.
Hearts not averse to being beguiled,   10
Beguile us in the way you know;
Release one leaf at break of day;
At noon release another leaf;
One from our trees, one far away;
Retard the sun with gentle mist;   15
Enchant the land with amethyst.
Slow, slow!
For the grapes' sake, if they were all,
Whose leaves already are burnt with frost,
Whose clustered fruit must else be lost—   20
For the grapes' sake along the wall.

Guiding Questions

1. The speaker plays upon two relevant meanings of the word "fall." What are they?
2. Lines 1-2 and 3-4 have a very different, contrasting tone. Analyze how this is achieved by: use of alliteration, word choice ("HUSHED" and "ripened," "wild" and "waste"), and assonance (the length and sound of the vowels).
3. Crows are birds with particular cultural connotations. What do they normally symbolize? Where will they "form and go"?
4. Why does the speaker want "the hours of this day [to be] slow ... less brief"? The day is obviously a day (and the days get shorter in autumn), but what might it symbolize?
5. To 'beguile' is to fool or trick. About what does the speaker want to be fooled? How could nature trick him? (Amethyst is a variety of quartz with a unique purple coloring. It has only positive connotations in cultures throughout the world.)
6. Comment on the effectiveness of line 17.
7. The adjective "clustered" personifies the grapes. What human action is suggested by it?

Final Thoughts

The seasons are almost universally seen as symbolic of the cycle of human life: spring = birth, summer = youth, fall = maturity, and winter = old age and death. Evidently the speaker sees himself as having reached maturity and senses the approach of death (represented by the leaves beginning to fall and the shortening days); therefore, he wants to savor every remaining moment. The poem speaks about the transient nature of life, but places it firmly in the context of the cycle of nature. Grapes are used to symbolize just how fragile life is since they are vulnerable to the cold. They cluster at the wall as though cowering together for protection, but one hard frost will kill them all. The association of grapes with wine and wine with life is traditional. Frost may have in mind Macbeth's statement on King Duncan's death, "The wine of life is drawn, and the mere lees / Is left this vault to brag of" (*Macbeth* 2.3).

34

Reluctance

Pre-reading:

How do you feel at the end of a really great vacation?
How do you feel when an important relationship comes to an end?

Out through the fields and the woods
And over the walls I have wended
I have climbed the hills of view
And looked at the world, and descended
I have come by the highway home   5
And lo, it is ended

The leaves are all dead on the ground
Save those that the oak is keeping
To ravel them one by one
And let them go scraping and creeping   10
Out over the crusted snow
When others are sleeping

And the dead leaves lie huddled and still
No longer blown hither and thither
The last lone aster is gone   15
The flowers of the witch-hazel wither
The heart is still aching to seek
But the feet question 'Whither'

Ah, when to the heart of man
Was it ever less than a treason   20
To go with the drift of things
To yield with a grace to reason
And bow and accept the end
Of a love or a season?

Guiding Questions
Lines 1-6:
1. What is important about the verb tense in the first verse? How are the verbs given emphasis? 2. What details suggest that the speaker has, during his journey, quite literally risen above the life that he had at home? What might this symbolize?

3. He writes that he has "come by the highway home." How does this contrast with the details of his journey that you have just commented upon?

4. Comment on the effect produced by the alliteration of the letter 'w' in lines 1-2 and 'h' in line

5. Comment on the impact of the short line 5. How does its rhythm work on you as reader?

Lines 7-18:
6. What season of the year is it? How do you know? [Note: Confusingly, the verb 'to ravel' can mean both 'to tangle' and 'to untangle.' Here, it means the latter.]

7. In what ways does the speaker feel himself to be like the leaves described in verses two and three and the flowers of the witch-hazel and aster in verse three? What distinction is he making between his spirit ("heart') and his body ("the feet")?

8. What exactly is the question that the speaker's feet ask on line 18?

Lines 19-24:
9. How would you describe the theme and the tone of the final verse? How are they different from the theme and the tone of the rest of the poem? How is this difference achieved?

Holistic:
10. This poem is divided into four stanzas of six lines each with three-stress lines except for the last-lines in each stanza which have two stresses. The rhyme scheme for each stanza is ABCBDB. What does the poet's use of rhyme add to your experience of the poem?

11. What is the "Reluctance" of the title?

Final Thoughts

It appears that Frost wrote this poem following the rejection of his proposal of marriage (one of several) by Elinor, the woman who would eventually become his wife. Dejected, perhaps even contemplating suicide, Frost returned home to Lawrence, Massachusetts where he lived with his mother and sister. As always, such autobiographical background is valuable in understanding the poem but does not limit the reader's interpretation of it.

This is the last poem in Frost's first published collection and it is in many ways an answer to the first, "Into My Own." In that poem, the speaker expresses his determination to turn his back on his home and travel beyond the world of highways on a quest for self-discovery. In "Reluctance" we see the speaker returning home to find nothing left for him but the dead leaves of the late autumn and winter seasons.

For a moment, the speaker is overwhelmed by the conviction that his quest has been pointless: he has achieved nothing by it and yet he appears unable to return to the world he once abandoned – there is nothing for him there, everything is dead. Then he picks himself up. He will not allow his life to be ruled by "the drift of things" nor will he "yield with a grace to reason" by accepting failure. As the Welsh poet Dylan Thomas wrote, he will, "Rage, rage against the dying of the light" ("Do not go gentle into that good night") – to do less would be to deny the human spirit.

North of Boston (1914)

Introduction

Following the financial, popular and critical success of *A Boy's Will*, David Nutt and Company was anxious to publish a second collection. The result was *North of Boston* published on May 15th, 1914 in Britain. The volume included some poems written as early as 1905 and others written since Frost's move to England. The reviews were very positive highlighting Frost's skill in making poetry out of the natural speech of New England folk and the realities of their lives. However, in February 1915, the year after the outbreak of World War I (July 28th, 1914 – November 11th, 1918), Frost returned with his family to America, where he bought a farm in Franconia, New Hampshire. In America, Henry Holt and Company had published *North of Boston* in 1914 and because of its success republished *A Boy's Will* in 1915. Both collections were enthusiastically received by critics and readers. When Frost went to England, he was virtually unknown as a poet; when he returned to the States, he came as an American poet with an international standing.

Originally titled *Farm Servants and Other People*, *North of Boston* had the subtitle "To E. M. F. [his wife Elinor Miriam White]: This Book of People." Together these two titles indicate what the final title (a phrase commonly used by realtors advertising properties for sale in the *Boston Globe* newspaper) does not: this collection moves beyond the introspection of *A Boy's Will*. The poems are arranged chronologically going through the seasons of a single year.

"The Pasture" was originally the introductory poem in this collection, but in 1923 Frost chose it to open the *Selected Poems of Robert Frost*. Subsequently, it appeared as the prologue to all of the selected and collected editions of his poetry and Frost often led off his readings with it as a way of introducing both himself and his poetry.

The Pasture

The poem was published in italic print as was the last poem in the collection "Good Hours" in order to establish their role as prologue and afterword to the collection.

Pre-reading

Ever needed desperately to share a particular experience with another person? Why?

I'm going out to clean the pasture spring;
I'll only stop to rake the leaves away
(And wait to watch the water clear, I may):
I sha'n't be gone long. – You come too.

I'm going out to fetch the little calf   5
That's standing by the mother. It's so young,
It totters when she licks it with her tongue.
I sha'n't be gone long. – You come too.

Guiding Questions

1. What do you know about the speaker in this poem? To whom do you think he is speaking? What is your evidence?

2. What season of the year is it? What do the activities described in verse one and verse two have in common? How does each establish regeneration and new life as a key theme of the poem?

3. The poem contains two quatrains with the rhyme scheme ABBC DEEC. Actually, the last line of each quatrain is simply repeated as a refrain. The meter is iambic pentameter except for the refrain line where the caesura (the pause between the two sentences) occurs in the middle of the third foot disrupting the pattern of iambic feet. However else you choose to scan the refrain line, "long" and "You" are stressed syllables breaking the pattern of stressed/unstressed. How does this structure add to the experience of reading the poem?

4. Which lines in the poem make effective use of alliteration? Comment on the effect produced by the sound of the lines you chose.

5. Comment on the importance of vowel sounds in the poem. (Clue: Long or short; harsh or soft? Why?)

6. The language of the poem is colloquial – it is not written in the heightened language of poetry but in the language that real New Englander's used. What does this colloquialism add to your experience of reading the poem?

7. Frost said of this poem: "the Sound in the mouths of men I found to be the basis of all effective expression, – not merely words or phrases, but sentences, – living things flying round, – the vital parts of speech. And my poems are to be read in the appreciative tones of this live speech" (Lecture Frost at the Browne & Nichols School in 1915, quoted in *Robert Frost On Writing* by Elaine Barry, Rutgers University Press, 1973). How does this comment affect your reading of this poem?

Final Thoughts

"The Pasture" functions as Frost's invitation to the reader to join him in experiencing his poetry collection. Kendall points out that, "Just as Greek antiquity associated the [poetic] Muses with springs, so Frost locates and tends the pastoral source of his poetic inspiration in his own 'pasture spring'" (47). Writing and reading poetry has the potential of achieving clarity and fresh insight (by raking away the dead leaves that clog the mind) if only both writer and reader have the patience to "watch the water clear."

The setting is springtime. The dead time of winter has passed and the time of rebirth is here. Stanza one emphasizes cleaning out the dead stuff that block the stream of creativity and stanza two emphasizes bringing something new into being and nurturing its growth. The "little calf" (symbol of rebirth) is a new poem growing in the writer's mind, so fragile that it "totters" when its mother (the poet) "licks it with her tongue." The farmer knows the joys of the two tasks he is leaving his loved one to perform, but he does not want to leave her – he wants to share that experience with her. Similarly, the poet knows the joys of poetic creation and wants to share these with the reader.

Mending Wall

"'Mending Wall' takes up the theme where 'A [sic] Tuft of Flowers' in A Boy's Will laid it down" (Frost's original authorial note).

Pre-reading

Make a list of the different kinds of walls and boundaries you can think of. Include both physical constructions and psychological barriers. What are the positive functions of such boundaries? What are their negatives? What limits do you set yourself to keep other people from getting too close to your private space?

SOMETHING there is that doesn't love a wall,
That sends the frozen-ground-swell under it,
And spills the upper boulders in the sun;
And makes gaps even two can pass abreast.
The work of hunters is another thing: 5
I have come after them and made repair
Where they have left not one stone on stone,
But they would have the rabbit out of hiding,
To please the yelping dogs. The gaps I mean,
No one has seen them made or heard them made,   10
But at spring mending-time we find them there.
I let my neighbor know beyond the hill;
And on a day we meet to walk the line
And set the wall between us once again.
We keep the wall between us as we go.   15
To each the boulders that have fallen to each.
And some are loaves and some so nearly balls
We have to use a spell to make them balance:
"Stay where you are until our backs are turned!"
We wear our fingers rough with handling them.   20
Oh, just another kind of outdoor game,
One on a side. It comes to little more:
He is all pine and I am apple-orchard.
My apple trees will never get across

42

And eat the cones under his pines, I tell him.   25
He only says, "Good fences make good neighbors."
Spring is the mischief in me, and I wonder
If I could put a notion in his head:
"Why do they make good neighbors? Isn't it
Where there are cows? But here there are no cows.   30
Before I built a wall I'd ask to know
What I was walling in or walling out,
And to whom I was like to give offence.
Something there is that doesn't love a wall,
That wants it down!" I could say "Elves" to him,   35
But it's not elves exactly, and I'd rather
He said it for himself. I see him there,
Bringing a stone grasped firmly by the top
In each hand, like an old-stone savage armed.
He moves in darkness as it seems to me,   40
Not of woods only and the shade of trees.
He will not go behind his father's saying,
And he likes having thought of it so well
He says again, "Good fences make good neighbors."

Guiding Questions

The questions are thematic rather than chronological:
1. The poem describes two New England farmers who come together each spring to walk on their side of the dry-stone wall (i.e., one made by balancing stones without cement) which marks the shared boundary of their fields and to replace the fallen stones. Why do they do this at this same time every year – why not in autumn? (Think of more than one reason.) What does each farmer produce in his field?
2. This poem is a dramatic monologue. The speaker's attitude to walls in general (and to the wall that needs repair in particular) is opposite from that of his neighbor. Highlight in one color the lines in which the speaker expresses his views and in another color his account of his neighbor's opinion on walls.
[Note: There is solid evidence that this is an autobiographical poem. Frost's

neighbor in New Hampshire had been a French-Canadian named Napoleon Guay, and the two had often walked together repaired the wall that separated their fields. The statement, "Good fences make good neighbors" was an adage that Guay often repeated. None of this, however, means that Frost is identical with the speaker in this poem. The adage or saying itself can be traced back to the American colonial period and even further back (in a variety of forms) to European and other cultures throughout the world. When humans were nomadic hunter-gatherers there was no need for barriers, but as soon as society transitioned to farming and herding, walls were needed to keeps the domesticated animals out of the crops and to demarcate one man's crops from those of another. [This was one of the cultural differences that caused great misunderstanding and friction between European settlers in America and the native people.] When, back in prehistory, humans came together to live in towns these were soon surrounded by defensive walls. Frost himself wrote in a letter dated May 1932, "(I am) in favor of a skin and fences and tariff walls" (quoted in Fagan 221).]

3. Let's explore the speaker's point of view. Bear in mind that he finds in wall mending an opportunity for social intercourse. What he values is the *process* of building the wall, not the end result, which he thinks is pretty pointless:

> Lines 1-4: Nature itself is without boundaries; it is man who, in his attempt to master nature, imposes boundaries upon it. What natural forces are involved in the destruction of the wall that is described here? Why do you think that the speaker uses the word "Something" at the start of the poem? What words would *you* use to describe the motivating force(s) he has in mind?

> Lines 5-9: In what ways is "The work of hunters" an entirely different form of destruction from that described in lines 1-4?

> Line 10: How does the detail in this line relate back to lines 1-4?

> Lines 11-14: Given the speaker's apparent attitude to building walls, what details in these lines are surprising? Can you reconcile these two things?

> Lines 16-22: How does the speaker's description of the ways that the two men go about remaking the wall stress its light-hearted, game-like quality? Why is it important to the speaker to portray the activity in this way?

> Lines 17-26: In these lines the speaker includes four reasons against

rebuilding the wall (lines 17-19, 20, 21-22 and 23-26). What are they?

Lines 32-34: What kind of "offense" could a wall give? (Not the pun on the word 'fence'!)

Lines 36-38: For what reasons does the speaker not identify the force that wants walls down as "'Elves'"?

Lines 38-40: What image is used by the speaker to describe his neighbor? What point is the speaker making by this comparison? Does it in any way undermine his attitude to walls?

Lines 41-42: What do you think that the word "darkness" means in this line? How does it link with the image in line 40?

Lines 43-45: What is the speaker's final criticism of his neighbor's desire to keep the wall between them?

4. So far it seems as though the speaker's point of view is the one supported in the poem. Be careful! We have to ask whether the poet identifies himself with the speaker or not. (Remember that in a dramatic monologue the character of the speaker is as much an invention of the writer as is a character in a play – hence the word 'dramatic'. Frost himself once commented, "I make it a rule not to take any 'character's' side in anything I write.") Let's explore some aspects of the poem that tend to undercut the speaker's opinion:

Explain how the way the poem is written gives particular power to the neighbor's statement, "'Good fences make good neighbors.'"

Lines 11-14: In what ways does the speaker's behavior contradict his attitude to the wall? Consider the irony that wall-building is clearly a communal act that gives the speaker an opportunity to meet and to interact with his neighbor – and (it appears) to have fun. After all, it is the speaker who contacts his neighbor to set up the meeting at the wall! [Consider particularly the poet's use of the word "meet" on line 13.]

Lines 15-22: What indication is there in these lines that rebuilding the wall is enjoyable?

5. What is the evidence that the narrator is as stuck in his way of seeing walls as he accuses his neighbor of being? You may want to bear in mind Frost's statement: "Poetry provides one permissible way of saying one thing and meaning another" ("Education by Poetry" 1931). Consider the ambiguity of the title "Mending Wall." Does it describe the activity of rebuilding the wall (i.e., 'mending' is a verb) or is it the wall that is strengthening the relationship between the two men (i.e., 'mending' is an adjective describing 'wall'). Perhaps, like the speaker, the poet introduces

"mischief" into the poem to make the reader think for him/herself.)
Holistic

6. The poem is written in blank verse (just like Shakespeare, a ten-syllable line arranged in five iambic feet without a regular rhyme scheme – hence the verse is 'blank'). Each line has five stressed syllables, but a rigid iambic beat. The rhythms are those of natural speech. Can you find the lines that have eleven syllables? Is there any significance in these being the longest lines in the poem?

7. What other features of the way the poem is written reflect the way people actually speak?

Final Thoughts

"The Tuft of Flowers" ends with the speaker's assertion of his new-found understanding that he is working "together" with the mower, because he is able to empathize with him, although in terms of time and place they are working "apart." This poem explores the opposite of this situation: the two men are working together in time and space, but they are not motivated by the same feelings about the task they are performing – in fact, they argue about it. Paradoxically, the two men are brought together by the task of remaking the wall that keeps them apart. The poem marks the clash of two aphorisms: "Good fences make good neighbors" and "Something there is that doesn't love a wall." Each man repeats his credo twice.

On a superficial reading, it appears that the speaker wins the debate hands down. His is a viewpoint with which the reader instinctively sympathizes. This is because everything is presented from his point of view. The only thing we hear from the other farmer is his mechanical repetition of words that are not even his but his father's. In contrast, the speaker not only has the freedom to point out that, given the use to which the adjacent fields are being put, a wall makes no logical sense at all, but also to provide a patronizing caricature of his neighbor as an uncivilized caveman. However, ambiguity is the essence of this poem. The speaker may *think* that he is absolutely against walls, but the poem shows otherwise. It is, after all, the speaker who contacts his neighbor every year to arrange the time for wall mending, and it is he who turns it into a game that he appears thoroughly to enjoy. He also takes full advantage of the social contact to do a lot of talking, as though he has been starved of social intercourse all winter. It seems that wall-making is a socially 'mending' activity. Thus in the poem, Frost raises the pros and cons and leaves the confused reader to sort out where he/she stands now.

The SparkNotes Editors make an interesting connection between the carefully built and re-built barrier in this poem, whose ostensible purpose is to confine, and Frost's rejection of free verse poetry in favor of writing in traditional (confining) poetic forms. Paradoxically, for some people barriers that offer "challenging frameworks within which to work" can (like the net in tennis) encourage individual self-expression and greater communication ("SparkNote on Frost's Early Poems"). This seems to me a very fruitful way of looking at this poem.

The Death of the Hired Man

Pre-reading

Ever been let down badly by someone you were counting on? What happened? How did you feel? What happened to your relationship with that person?

MARY sat musing on the lamp-flame at the table
Waiting for Warren. When she heard his step,
She ran on tip-toe down the darkened passage
To meet him in the doorway with the news
And put him on his guard. "Silas is back."   5
She pushed him outward with her through the door
And shut it after her. "Be kind," she said.
She took the market things from Warren's arms
And set them on the porch, then drew him down
To sit beside her on the wooden steps.   10

"When was I ever anything but kind to him?
But I'll not have the fellow back," he said.
"I told him so last haying, didn't I?
'If he left then,' I said, 'that ended it.'
What good is he? Who else will harbour him   15
At his age for the little he can do?
What help he is there's no depending on.
Off he goes always when I need him most.
'He thinks he ought to earn a little pay,
Enough at least to buy tobacco with,   20
So he won't have to beg and be beholden.'
'All right,' I say, 'I can't afford to pay
Any fixed wages, though I wish I could.'
'Someone else can.' 'Then someone else will have to.'
I shouldn't mind his bettering himself   25
If that was what it was. You can be certain,
When he begins like that, there's someone at him
Trying to coax him off with pocket-money, –
In haying time, when any help is scarce.

In winter he comes back to us. I'm done."   30

"Sh! not so loud: he'll hear you," Mary said.

"I want him to: he'll have to soon or late."

"He's worn out. He's asleep beside the stove.
When I came up from Rowe's I found him here,
Huddled against the barn-door fast asleep,   35
A miserable sight, and frightening, too –
You needn't smile – I didn't recognise him –
I wasn't looking for him – and he's changed.
Wait till you see."

"Where did you say he'd been?"

"He didn't say. I dragged him to the house,   40
And gave him tea and tried to make him smoke.
I tried to make him talk about his travels.
Nothing would do: he just kept nodding off."

"What did he say? Did he say anything?"

"But little."

"Anything? Mary, confess   45
He said he'd come to ditch the meadow for me."

"Warren!"

"But did he? I just want to know."

"Of course he did. What would you have him say?
Surely you wouldn't grudge the poor old man
Some humble way to save his self-respect.   50
He added, if you really care to know,
He meant to clear the upper pasture, too.
That sounds like something you have heard before?

49

Warren, I wish you could have heard the way
He jumbled everything. I stopped to look 55
Two or three times – he made me feel so queer –
To see if he was talking in his sleep.
He ran on Harold Wilson – you remember –
The boy you had in haying four years since.
He's finished school, and teaching in his college. 60
Silas declares you'll have to get him back.
He says they two will make a team for work:
Between them they will lay this farm as smooth!
The way he mixed that in with other things.
He thinks young Wilson a likely lad, though daft 65
On education – you know how they fought
All through July under the blazing sun,
Silas up on the cart to build the load,
Harold along beside to pitch it on."

"Yes, I took care to keep well out of earshot." 70

"Well, those days trouble Silas like a dream.
You wouldn't think they would. How some things linger!
Harold's young college boy's assurance piqued him.
After so many years he still keeps finding
Good arguments he sees he might have used. 75
I sympathise. I know just how it feels
To think of the right thing to say too late.
Harold's associated in his mind with Latin.
He asked me what I thought of Harold's saying
He studied Latin like the violin 80
Because he liked it – that an argument!
He said he couldn't make the boy believe
He could find water with a hazel prong –
Which showed how much good school had ever done him.
He wanted to go over that. But most of all 85
He thinks if he could have another chance
To teach him how to build a load of hay——"

"I know, that's Silas' one accomplishment.

He bundles every forkful in its place,
And tags and numbers it for future reference,   90
So he can find and easily dislodge it
In the unloading. Silas does that well.
He takes it out in bunches like big birds' nests.
You never see him standing on the hay
He's trying to lift, straining to lift himself."   95

"He thinks if he could teach him that, he'd be
Some good perhaps to someone in the world.
He hates to see a boy the fool of books.
Poor Silas, so concerned for other folk,
And nothing to look backward to with pride,   100
And nothing to look forward to with hope,
So now and never any different."

Part of a moon was falling down the west,
Dragging the whole sky with it to the hills.
Its light poured softly in her lap. She saw   105
And spread her apron to it. She put out her hand
Among the harp-like morning-glory strings,
Taut with the dew from garden bed to eaves,
As if she played unheard the tenderness
That wrought on him beside her in the night.   110
"Warren," she said, "he has come home to die:
You needn't be afraid he'll leave you this time."

"Home," he mocked gently.

"Yes, what else but home?
It all depends on what you mean by home.
Of course he's nothing to us, any more   115
Than was the hound that came a stranger to us
Out of the woods, worn out upon the trail."

"Home is the place where, when you have to go there,
They have to take you in."

"I should have called it
Something you somehow haven't to deserve."   120

Warren leaned out and took a step or two,
Picked up a little stick, and brought it back
And broke it in his hand and tossed it by.
"Silas has better claim on us you think
Than on his brother? Thirteen little miles   125
As the road winds would bring him to his door.
Silas has walked that far no doubt to-day.
Why didn't he go there? His brother's rich,
A somebody – director in the bank."

"He never told us that."

"We know it though."   130

"I think his brother ought to help, of course.
I'll see to that if there is need. He ought of right
To take him in, and might be willing to –
He may be better than appearances.
But have some pity on Silas. Do you think   135
If he'd had any pride in claiming kin
Or anything he looked for from his brother,
He'd keep so still about him all this time?"

"I wonder what's between them."

"I can tell you.
Silas is what he is – we wouldn't mind him –   140
But just the kind that kinsfolk can't abide.
He never did a thing so very bad.
He don't know why he isn't quite as good
As anyone. He won't be made ashamed
To please his brother, worthless though he is."   145

"*I* can't think Si ever hurt anyone."

"No, but he hurt my heart the way he lay
And rolled his old head on that sharp-edged chair-back.
He wouldn't let me put him on the lounge.
You must go in and see what you can do.   150
I made the bed up for him there to-night.
You'll be surprised at him – how much he's broken.
His working days are done; I'm sure of it."

"I'd not be in a hurry to say that."

"I haven't been. Go, look, see for yourself.   155
But, Warren, please remember how it is:
He's come to help you ditch the meadow.
He has a plan. You mustn't laugh at him.
He may not speak of it, and then he may.
I'll sit and see if that small sailing cloud   160
Will hit or miss the moon."

It hit the moon.
Then there were three there, making a dim row,
The moon, the little silver cloud, and she.

Warren returned – too soon, it seemed to her,
Slipped to her side, caught up her hand and waited.   165

"Warren," she questioned.

"Dead," was all he answered.

Guiding Questions

This poem is a dramatic lyric which, like a play, presents a continuous scene with spoken dialogue as well as plot narrative and description. Kendall comments, "Written around 1905 and collected almost a decade later in *North of Boston*, "The Death of the Hired Man" marked a shift into poetry as a drama of everyday lives – and deaths" (6). The unexpected return of Silas (the elderly hired farmhand of the title), who has in the past on more than one occasion abused Warren's trust, loyalty, and patience, leads to conflict between the farmer and his wife, Mary, who is much more forgiving of Silas' former misconduct because she is convinced that he has come back to the farm to die. At the time of their publication, "The Death of the Hired Man" and "Home Burial" represented an original poetic genre by presenting a drama in the natural speech rhythms of the ordinary people of New England.

Silas is a farm laborer of a kind becoming less common at the time the poem was written as agriculture became increasingly mechanized and run as a business. In this way, the poem is not simply about the passing of an individual but the passing of an era when farm production was mainly a manual occupation in which farmers worked alongside their hired men for long hours in the fields.

Lines 1 –10:

1. What does the word "musing" add to the opening of the poem that the synonym "thinking" would not have given?

2. Contrast the rhythm of lines two and three. In what ways are the rhythms different? Why are the rhythms different? How is the rhythm of each line created?

3. What effect is created by having Mary's first two pieces of dialogue so short and placed in the second half of the line following a long caesura (lines 5 and 7)?

4. There are five examples of alliteration, usually involving pairs of words: "MARY sat musing … Waiting for Warren … she heard his step, / She … on tip-toe … drew him down." What effect on tone and rhythm do four of these examples have? Which has a very different effect?

5. Mary asks her husband to "be kind" and then takes "the market things from Warren's arms." What might this action symbolize about the very different value systems of the two people? Mary and Warren have contrasting conceptions about what constitutes being 'kind' (as later they will have very different ideas about what constitutes 'home'). Explain what

each means by being "kind" to Silas. From Mary's actions and words, what would you speculate about Warren's feelings towards Silas?

Lines 11-30:

Note that when Silas has worked on Warren's farm in the past, Warren has not been able to pay him regular wages. Silas has worked for bed and board – and perhaps any little bonus that Warren could afford to give him once he sold his harvest.

6. What happened last haying which, Warren believes, put an end to his relationship with Silas and to any sense of obligation he might have felt for a fellow human being? Why does Warren feel so resentful about what happened? Along with the resentment, can you detect another, very different, feeling in Warren?

Lines 31-43:

5. What reasons does Mary give for her concern over Silas? Look at the rhythm of her speech. How is it different from the rhythm of Warren's speech? How does the poet achieve this different kind of speech? What is the reason for the difference?

Lines 44-52:

6. How is it that Warren can guess what Silas told his wife about his reason for returning? How does he react when Mary confirms that his guess was right?

7. Mary takes a very different view of the reason Silas gave. How does she interpret what the hired man said?

Lines 53-63:

8. What details of Silas' speech (as reported by Mary) indicate that he is not thinking clearly and logically?

9. What difference have you noticed thus far in how Warren and Mary refer to the hired man (i.e. the nouns they use)?

Lines 64-87

10. What did Silas resent about young Wilson? What did he also like and admire about him?

11. How is it that Mary understands just how Silas feels about his interactions with Wilson?

Lines 88-102:

12. What is entirely new and unexpected in the way Warren talks about Silas on lines 91 to 98?

13. What tragic dimension does Mary find in Silas' situation?

Lines 103-112:

14. How is Mary transformed in these lines? Analyze the simile of Mary seeming to play "the harp-like morning-glory strings." (Clue: Morning-Glory is "a vine that climbs by twisting around something and has large trumpet-shaped flowers that close in bright sunshine" [Merriam-Webster]. The flowers also open in the morning, hence the name. With what kind of being do you associate playing the harp?)

15. What effect is Mary having on Warren at this point?

16. Mary says, "'Warren, … he has come home to die:'" From what the reader has learned of Warren's attitude to Silas, how do you think he will react to Mary's use of the word "'home'"? What do you think Mary means by using this word (since the farm is obviously not literally Silas' home, and Mary and Warren are not kin [related] to him)?

Lines 113-138:

16. Explain the very different concepts that Warren and Mary have of what "home" means. How does this difference explain the way that each has reacted to Silas' return?

17. How does Mary explain why Silas does not go to his prosperous brother in his time of need? Why does Warren think that his brother is exactly where Silas should go?

18. Mary tells Warren, "'I think his brother ought to help, of course. / I'll see to that if there is need.'" What circumstances does she have in mind under which she would contact Silas' brother for help?

Lines 139-175

19. What do you find surprising about what Warren says on lines 146 and 154?

20. How does Mary account for the rift between Silas and his brother in terms of Silas' character?

21. Why does Mary consider it to be so important that when Warren sees, and presumably talks to, Silas he remembers that the hired man has returned "'to help you ditch the meadow'"?

22. Suggest why the half-line, "It hit the moon" is significant. Comment on the meaning of the lines, "Then there was three there, making a dim row, / The moon, the little silver cloud, and she."

23. How does the ending of the poem reflect the opening lines? What is the effect of this deliberate echoing on you?

Final Thoughts

The terms of Silas's contract with Warren (presumably verbal rather than written) were that he would take most of his pay in room and board with the family even in the months when there was little actual work to do on the farm, so as to be available at harvesting when labor is always scarce. He would not receive a regular wage, but would be paid after the harvest when Warren sold his crop. Silas has, however, repeatedly violated this 'gentleman's agreement' by leaving Warren to seek paid employment on other farms. This, together with the fact that he is now old and not capable of doing much heavy labor, is the reason why Warren will "not have the fellow back." Warren feels that he no longer has any obligation to provide Silas with food and board because he is applying a moral rule based on economics: the fair exchange of labor for reward. (What an economist would term a 'cost/benefit analysis.') Since Silas has broken his contract and no longer has labor to exchange, Warren feels that their relationship has ended and with it any responsibilities he might have to his former employee.

In contrast to her husband, Mary shows a compassionate willingness to help Silas simply because he is a fellow human being, not because he is entitled to or even deserving of help – in fact, for Mary the less Silas deserves help, the greater is the obligation upon herself and her husband to give it. As soon as she has told Warren of Silas' return, she exhorts him to "be kind" and then takes "the market things from Warren's arms." Symbolically, she is asking him to judge the old man on the basis of common humanity (or if you prefer Christian forgiveness) not on the basis of what economists call 'market forces.' Their different perspective is made clear in their contrasting definitions of home. To Warren, home is a place where obligations are set in stone by the accident of birth: brother has to care for brother because they are united in blood. But to Mary home is wherever people (and animals) are freely welcomed. Many critics, including Frost himself, identify Mary's view as the "feminine way of it, the mother way" and Warren's as "the male one" (*"Paris Review* Interview") – compassion contrasted with economics, giving contrasted with trading. The moon symbolism associates Mary with childbirth and fecundity. She is symbolically Warren's better angel exerting "some tenderness / ... on him beside her in the night."

Mary is the only one of the two who has actually seen the extent of Silas' illness and this is why she is initially the more compassionate. However, one senses that Warren is more empathetic than he likes to pretend (Silas has, after all, let himself down several times and been allowed back). By the end of the poem, his attitude to Silas has certainly softened which is an example of tragic irony because Silas ultimately dies alone rather than with his adoptive family and also without ever fulfilling his contract to ditch the meadow and clear the upper pasture.

Home Burial

Pre-reading

This poem deals with a topic we all struggle with. I do not know about you, but I simply cannot conceive of the grief parents must feel at the death of a child, particularly a young child. In *On Death and Dying* (1969) Elisabeth Kübler-Ross identified five stages of grief and loss: 1. Denial and isolation; 2. Anger; 3. Bargaining; 4. Depression; 5. Acceptance. However, not everyone who is grieving will go through the stages in the same order or experience all of them. If you have experienced intense grief, what did/do you feel? How did you cope?

HE saw her from the bottom of the stairs
Before she saw him. She was starting down,
Looking back over her shoulder at some fear.
She took a doubtful step and then undid it
To raise herself and look again. He spoke   5
Advancing toward her: "What is it you see
From up there always – for I want to know."
She turned and sank upon her skirts at that,
And her face changed from terrified to dull.
He said to gain time: "What is it you see,"   10
Mounting until she cowered under him.
"I will find out now – you must tell me, dear."
She, in her place, refused him any help
With the least stiffening of her neck and silence.
She let him look, sure that he wouldn't see,   15
Blind creature; and a while he didn't see.
But at last he murmured, "Oh," and again, "Oh."

"What is it – what?" she said.

"Just that I see."

"You don't," she challenged. "Tell me what it is."

"The wonder is I didn't see at once.   20
I never noticed it from here before.
I must be wonted to it – that's the reason.
The little graveyard where my people are!
So small the window frames the whole of it.
Not so much larger than a bedroom, is it?   25
There are three stones of slate and one of marble,
Broad-shouldered little slabs there in the sunlight
On the sidehill. We haven't to mind those.
But I understand: it is not the stones,
But the child's mound——"
"Don't, don't, don't, don't," she cried.   30

She withdrew shrinking from beneath his arm
That rested on the banister, and slid downstairs;
And turned on him with such a daunting look,
He said twice over before he knew himself:
"Can't a man speak of his own child he's lost?"   35

"Not you! Oh, where's my hat? Oh, I don't need it!
I must get out of here. I must get air.
I don't know rightly whether any man can."

"Amy! Don't go to someone else this time.
Listen to me. I won't come down the stairs."   40
He sat and fixed his chin between his fists.
"There's something I should like to ask you, dear."

"You don't know how to ask it."

"Help me, then."
Her fingers moved the latch for all reply.

"My words are nearly always an offence.   45
I don't know how to speak of anything
So as to please you. But I might be taught
I should suppose. I can't say I see how.
A man must partly give up being a man

With women-folk. We could have some arrangement   50
By which I'd bind myself to keep hands off
Anything special you're a-mind to name.
Though I don't like such things 'twixt those that love.
Two that don't love can't live together without them.
But two that do can't live together with them."   55
She moved the latch a little. "Don't – don't go.
Don't carry it to someone else this time.
Tell me about it if it's something human.
Let me into your grief. I'm not so much
Unlike other folks as your standing there   60
Apart would make me out. Give me my chance.
I do think, though, you overdo it a little.
What was it brought you up to think it the thing
To take your mother-loss of a first child
So inconsolably – in the face of love.   65
You'd think his memory might be satisfied——"

"There you go sneering now!"

"I'm not, I'm not!
You make me angry. I'll come down to you.
God, what a woman! And it's come to this,
A man can't speak of his own child that's dead."   70

"You can't because you don't know how.
If you had any feelings, you that dug
With your own hand – how could you? – his little grave;
I saw you from that very window there,
Making the gravel leap and leap in air   75
Leap up, like that, like that, and land so lightly
And roll back down the mound beside the hole.
I thought, Who is that man? I didn't know you.
And I crept down the stairs and up the stairs
To look again, and still your spade kept lifting.   80
Then you came in. I heard your rumbling voice
Out in the kitchen, and I don't know why,
But I went near to see with my own eyes.

You could sit there with the stains on your shoes
Of the fresh earth from your own baby's grave   85
And talk about your everyday concerns.
You had stood the spade up against the wall
Outside there in the entry, for I saw it."

"I shall laugh the worst laugh I ever laughed.
I'm cursed. God, if I don't believe I'm cursed."   90

"I can repeat the very words you were saying.
'Three foggy mornings and one rainy day
Will rot the best birch fence a man can build.'
Think of it, talk like that at such a time!
What had how long it takes a birch to rot   95
To do with what was in the darkened parlour.
You couldn't care! The nearest friends can go
With anyone to death, comes so far short
They might as well not try to go at all.
No, from the time when one is sick to death,   100
One is alone, and he dies more alone.
Friends make pretence of following to the grave,
But before one is in it, their minds are turned
And making the best of their way back to life
And living people, and things they understand.   105
But the world's evil. I won't have grief so
If I can change it. Oh, I won't, I won't!"

"There, you have said it all and you feel better.
You won't go now. You're crying. Close the door.
The heart's gone out of it: why keep it up.   110
Amy! There's someone coming down the road!"

"You – oh, you think the talk is all. I must go –
Somewhere out of this house. How can I make you—"

"If – you – do!" She was opening the door wider.
"Where do you mean to go? First tell me that.   115
I'll follow and bring you back by force. I will!—"

Guiding Questions

Frost had personal experience of the death of children. His first-born son, Elliott, died of cholera aged three in 1900. His daughter, Elinor Bettina, died just three days after her birth in 1907. Frost's own father had died of tuberculosis in 1885 when Frost was only 11.

Lines 1-16:

1. The woman is described as looking at "some fear." What indication is given of the woman's emotions as she stands on the stair? How is it made clear that she simply cannot free herself from the power of whatever it is that she is looking at?

2. Look carefully at the man's words on lines 6 to 12. What is it about the way he speaks that explains why the woman "cowered under him"?

3. When she realizes that her husband is at the foot of the stairs, the woman's expression changes "from terrified to dull." What does "dull" mean in this context? What does the change described suggest about relations between the husband and wife?

4. Throughout the poem, stanza breaks occur where quoted speech ends or begins. What effect does breaking up the line pattern in lines 17 to 19 produce?

5. The woman is at the top and the man at the bottom of the stairs which is a vivid visual image of the gulf between them. Examine the symbolism of their changing positions on the stairs.

6. Why does the wife think of her husband as a "Blind creature"? How does the description of his reaction as he looks out of the window prove that the phrase "Blind creature" might equally apply to his wife?

Lines 17-30

Notice the way the poet delays telling the reader just what it is that the man and wife can see from the top of the stairs.

7. The man suggests that he did not notice that the graveyard could be seen from the window because he is "wonted to it." What does he mean by this? What details in lines 20 to 30 support his explanation?

8. When the man looks out at the "little graveyard" he sees the totality of it as the place where generations of his people are. Explain what, in contrast, the woman sees when she looks out.

Lines 31-44:

9. Frost said that the repetition of the word 'don't' was "the supreme thing in [the poem]." Explain why you think he felt that.

10. Describe how the woman reacts when her husband speaks of "the child's

mound." What reasons does she give for the way she reacts?

11. At this point in the poem, the man is desperate to prevent his wife from leaving the house. Explain what he means when he begs her, "Don't take it to someone else this time." What is "it"?

Lines 45-66:

12. What suggestions does the man make about how they might adjust their life together to accommodate his wife's feelings? How sensitive is he being to the way she feels?

13. The man seems to think that what is coming between them is a basic difference between the sexes. ("Men are from Mars; women are from Venus" – that sort of thing.) To what extent do you feel that the poet wants the reader to agree with this?

14. The husband says, "'I do think, though, you overdo it a little.'" What does he think she is overdoing? Why does he think this? Is he right?

Lines 67-88:

15. What does the man say that makes his wife accuse him of "sneering"? Is his wife right? Was he?

16. What do we learn of why it is that the wife thinks that her husband has no right to speak "of his own child he's lost"? Look carefully at the way the woman describes his actions. How is her disapproval reflected in the way she describes what he did? (Clues: Look at the rhythms of her speech. Consider the alliteration on lines 75 to 76 and 84 and 87.)

17. Do you think that the wife is right in her judgment of her husband's actions in burying his little son and afterwards talking about his "everyday concerns"?

Lines 89-107:

18. What do you make of the man's outburst on lines 89-90? What does he mean by these words? What does his wife understand him to mean by them?

19. What conclusions did the woman draw from the man's talking about birch fencing? What was it that "'was in the darkened parlour'"? Explain the way in which "'how long it takes a birch to rot'" *was* very relevant in the man's mind to the death of his son.

20. What is it that makes the woman conclude that no one can comfort a person grieving for the death of a loved one, that grief is a time when "'One is alone'"? What is it that she really objects to in the grief of everyone other than herself – the thing that she shouts she won't "have … so"? Little calls this "an existential concern that we are all essentially alone" (107).

Lines 108-116

21. What makes the conclusion of the poem so dramatic?

22. In what ways does the man fail his wife in this section of the poem?

Holistic:

23. Do you find yourself more sympathetic to the woman or to the man? Why? Only when you have answered, read this: "[The poem] intends to portray a failure of empathy and communication. Each person fails to appreciate the other's grieving process – fails to credit it, allow it, and have patience with it. And each fails to alter even slightly his or her own form of grief in order to accommodate the other. The reader witnesses the breakdown of a marriage … but more basically, this is a breakdown of human communication" (SparkNotes Editors, "Frost's Early Poems"). How does this affect your understanding and appreciation of the poem?

24. Explore the possible meanings of the title "Home Burial." (Clue: There are at least two.)

Final Thoughts

This dramatic narrative is one of Frost's bleakest poems: the death of the couple's first-born son in infancy has led effectively to the death of their marriage, despite the fact that they once evidently loved each other very much. The farmer and his wife each grieve for their lost son in their own very personal way, but each fails to understand or empathize with the other's grieving process and so dialogue between them is virtually impossible (almost as though they were each speaking a different language that the other does not understand). To a large extent, this failure seems to originate in their gender. Faced with the death of his son, the father threw himself into physical work because as a farmer that is what he is used to doing – it took him mind off his loss. It is also important to him that he, not a stranger, should dig his child's grave and that the grave should be situated amongst the graves of his own family. As a farmer, he is used to the cycle of life and death, that is what his wife angrily condemns as his "'way-of-the-world'" mentality. In the midst of life there is death, but there is also the continuity of the family working the multi-generational farm – each life is part of a greater whole. For Amy, however, the death of her son is a moment that will always be *now*; for her there is no getting over it or getting past it, or going on with one's life. Doing so would seem to her an act of treachery to her dead son. Fagan writes, "The two repeat themselves in an attempt to make clear what they wish to communicate, but they are incapable of communicating what they feel, no matter how many times they repeat themselves" (156). Because each fails entirely to understand the other, they fail to offer comfort. Everything he says and does is to Amy precisely the wrong thing, and to him she is simply indulging in emotions rather than getting hold of herself. The dash that ends the poem suggests that the conflict between the two is unresolved. The poem's ending which is not ending is ambiguous: the reader is left to speculate on what happens.

After Apple-Picking

Pre-reading

Think of a time when you had worked very hard at some physical task and went to bed aching and exhausted. What were your thoughts as you drifted off to sleep?

Note that the sequence and tenses of the poem are a bit confusing and lead the reader to wonder what is dreamed, what is real, and where the sleep begins. This is deliberate since it accurately reflects the consciousness of the speaker.

My long two-pointed ladder's sticking through a tree
Toward heaven still,
And there's a barrel that I didn't fill
Beside it, and there may be two or three
Apples I didn't pick upon some bough.   5
But I am done with apple-picking now.
Essence of winter sleep is on the night,
The scent of apples: I am drowsing off.
I cannot rub the strangeness from my sight
I got from looking through a pane of glass   10
I skimmed this morning from the drinking trough
And held against the world of hoary grass.
It melted, and I let it fall and break.
But I was well
Upon my way to sleep before it fell,   15
And I could tell
What form my dreaming was about to take.
Magnified apples appear and disappear,
Stem end and blossom end,
And every fleck of russet showing clear.   20
My instep arch not only keeps the ache,
It keeps the pressure of a ladder-round.

I feel the ladder sway as the boughs bend.
And I keep hearing from the cellar bin
The rumbling sound   25
Of load on load of apples coming in.
For I have had too much
Of apple-picking: I am overtired
Of the great harvest I myself desired.
There were ten thousand thousand fruit to touch,   30
Cherish in hand, lift down, and not let fall.
For all
That struck the earth,
No matter if not bruised or spiked with stubble,
Went surely to the cider-apple heap   35
As of no worth.
One can see what will trouble
This sleep of mine, whatever sleep it is.
Were he not gone,
The woodchuck could say whether it's like his   40
Long sleep, as I describe its coming on,
Or just some human sleep.

Guiding Questions

Holistic

1. Little writes that this poem, "is the wrenching depiction of someone on the verge of existential collapse. He has worked himself to exhaustion and is giving up, noting that there may be a little work left to do, but he is not going to do it ... That final melancholy exhaustion may be the key to why the poem is so cherished and highly respected" (115). He expands on this later writing, "The poem is not solely about a man tired of picking apples; rather, it presents a man tired because we all live and work in an imperfect world in which efforts expended often accomplish little change or discernible result" (118). As you read through the poem, and as you re-read it, keep this judgment in mind and consider whether it captures your own understanding of and experience of the poem. (Remember that critics can be right and critics can be wrong.)

Lines 1-6:

2. From what perspective does the speaker appear to be viewing the scene that he describes? (Clue: Consider the verb tense, the tone and the mood of the writing.)

Line 7-8:

3. What does the speaker mean by the phrase, "Essence of winter sleep"?

Lines 9-15:

4. What incident from the morning does the speaker remember in his last few moments of consciousness before falling into an exhausted sleep? How does the description suggest the coming of winter?

Lines 16-26:

5. From the description in these lines, how can you tell that the speaker is dreaming?

Lines 27-29:

6. What paradox does the speaker point out?

Lines 30-36:

7. Which words suggest the care that the picker took? Comment on the contrast between this language and the words used to describe the rejected apples ("bruised ... spiked ... heap ... no worth").

Lines 37-42:

Note: The woodchuck, or groundhog, is a rodent of the ground squirrel family. Groundhogs are true hibernators and build a special burrow in which to spend winter.

8. What would be the difference between the woodchuck's "Long sleep"

and "just some human sleep"?

9. Some critics suggest that the "Long sleep" is the sleep of death. How does this suggestion affect your understanding of the poem?

Holistic:

10. "There are many other things I have found myself saying about poetry, but the chiefest of these is that it is metaphor, saying one thing and meaning another, saying one thing in terms of another, the pleasure of ulteriority." ['Ulteriority' (noun) is a real word, but most dictionaries unhelpfully define it as "the quality of being ulterior." It means: 'Saying something that has a double meaning because one is saying one thing in terms of another.'] This is Robert Frost in 1946 from an essay for *The Atlantic Monthly*. With this statement in mind, do you think this is simply a poem about apple picking or does it have a deeper symbolic meaning? What might be symbolized by: apple picking, the apples that go to the cider heap, the approaching winter, and the speaker's on-coming sleep?

11. Consider the following interpretation of the symbolism of the poem: "Apple picking, in Western civilization, has its own built-in metaphorical and allegorical universe … When the poet speaks of 'the great harvest I myself desired,' consider also what apples represent in *Genesis*: knowledge and some great, punishable claim to godliness – creation and understanding, perhaps. This sends us scurrying back to lines 1 and 2, where the apple-picking ladder sticks through the tree 'Toward heaven still.' What has this harvest been, then, with its infinite fruits too many for one person to touch? What happens when such apples strike the earth – are they really of no worth? And looked at in this new light, what does it mean to be 'done with apple-picking now'?" (SparkNotes Editors, "Frost's Early Poems"). How helpful do you find this account of the poem's possible metaphorical interpretations?

12. Comment on the effectiveness of the poet's use of lines of varied length.

13. This is a poem in which all 42 lines end with full rhymes. However, the pattern of rhyme changes to reflect the feelings of the speaker: lines 1 to 12: ABBACCDEDFEF; lines 13 to 26: GHHHGIJIGKJLKL; lines 27 to 32: MNNMOO; lines 33 to 42: PQRPQSTSTR. Of course, the rhyming patterns work in conjunction with the patterns of the poem's meter, the use of enjambment and short lines, and the rhythms these create. Almost two thirds of the lines are standard iambic pentameter, but that leaves a lot of lines that are irregular. The disruption to the stressed/unstressed pattern of the syllables, particularly when the poet introduces a short line, reflects the loss

of control felt by the speaker as he falls into a sleep haunted by dreams of apple picking. Analyze the poet's use of rhyme and rhythm to convey to the reader the speaker's feelings and mood.

Final Thoughts

Though it has remained one of Frost's most popular poems, "After Apple Picking" has a surreal quality that is unusual in Frost which makes it difficult for the reader to distinguish actual experience from dream. Also, more typically of Frost, the poem hints at deeper, metaphorical meanings, but critics have disagreed on what these might be. On the literal level, the poem poses no problems: exhausted by days and days of apple picking after a bumper harvest, the speaker drifts into a deep sleep in which he dreams of … picking apples. This is an experience with which every reader can empathize: being so dog-tired that it's difficult to see straight or to say where reality ends and dreaming begins. That, I think, is the reason for the poem's popularity.

First let us clarify what actually happens in the poem as this is frequently misunderstood. The poem opens with the speaker in bed (presumably) just about to go to sleep. He remembers being in the apple orchard having just come down the ladder with a bucket full of perfect, unbruised apples and looking up at his ladder in the tree. He reflects that this was the moment when he decided he was "done with apple-picking" despite the fact that there may still have been a few stray apples unpicked and an apple barrel that was not full. His sleepiness makes him feel at one with nature because, "Essence of winter sleep is on the night": he and the earth seem to be shutting down together. The earth is preparing for the sleep of winter, and he is also going to sleep (not just because he is going to sleep that night but because winter will mean an end to activity on the farm).

Still approaching the borders of sleep, the speaker recalls having skimmed off a thin sheet of ice from the water trough that morning – perhaps the first ice on the trough that autumn and therefore the first indication of approaching winter. He recalls that he held the ice in front of his face and looked through it. Not surprisingly (since ice does not have the uniform composition of glass) the 'lens' of the ice distorted the image of the world. Now he finds that he "cannot rub the strangeness from my sight." Presumably his exhaustion means that he still sees the world as distorted, or more figuratively, he means that he cannot get the reality of the coming winter out of his head. He further recalls that he let the ice sheet melt in his hands, fall to the ground and shatter. Then he says, "But I was well / Upon my way to sleep before it fell." This line has caused some confusion. He means that, as he is recalling the incident he drifts off toward sleep before he gets to the part in his recollection where he drops the ice.

Now in that uncertain state oscillating between wakefulness and sleep, the speaker describes the dreams he knows he will have – almost a nightmare of a harvest so bountiful that it outstrips his physical strength. Finally, before he loses consciousness, the speaker wonders if this sleep will be "just some human sleep," seven to nine hours and then he will get up and get on with things, or like the woodchuck's hibernation, a 'sleep' of months when there is no work to do on the farm.

Metaphorical interpretations of the poem abound. Sleep is often seen as a euphemism for death (for example the final two lines of "Stopping by Woods on a Snowy Evening"). On this reading, the bumper harvest stands for a life spent working (in this case on a farm) which must end at some point when the body just gets too tired and worn out to go on. At that point, even the most fulfilled individual must think of tasks not completed and goals not attained, before slipping, with a sense of the rightness of the cycle of birth and death, into unconsciousness. Apple harvesting might also be understood as a metaphor for poetic creation – a form of consciousness above the normal – a striving "Toward heaven still." On this reading, the poem is about coming back to down to earth from the heightened consciousness of artistic creation, and much that has just been written above applies also to this situation. Some critics have made the inevitable connection between picking apples and the Garden of Eden, but I have not found this approach to be helpful in understanding the poem. You may find it more productive.

The Wood-Pile

Pre-Reading

Ever come across something made a long time ago by another person whom you do not know? (A diary or poem perhaps, or a painting, a needlework sampler, etc.) How did it make you feel?

Out walking in the frozen swamp one gray day,
I paused and said, "I will turn back from here.
No, I will go on farther – and we shall see."
The hard snow held me, save where now and then
One foot went through. The view was all in lines   5
Straight up and down of tall slim trees
Too much alike to mark or name a place by
So as to say for certain I was here
Or somewhere else: I was just far from home.
A small bird flew before me. He was careful   10
To put a tree between us when he lighted,
And say no word to tell me who he was
Who was so foolish as to think what he thought.
He thought that I was after him for a feather –
The white one in his tail; like one who takes   15
Everything said as personal to himself.
One flight out sideways would have undeceived him.
And then there was a pile of wood for which
I forgot him and let his little fear
Carry him off the way I might have gone,   20
Without so much as wishing him good-night.
He went behind it to make his last stand.
It was a cord of maple, cut and split
And piled – and measured, four by four by eight.
And not another like it could I see.   25

No runner tracks in this year's snow looped near it.
And it was older sure than this year's cutting,
Or even last year's or the year's before.
The wood was gray and the bark warping off it
And the pile somewhat sunken. Clematis   30
Had wound strings round and round it like a bundle.
What held it, though, on one side was a tree
Still growing, and on one side a stake for a prop,
These latter about to fall. I thought that only
Someone who lived in turning to fresh tasks   35
Could so forget his handiwork on which
He spent himself, the labor of his ax,
And leave it there far from a useful fireplace
To warm the frozen swamp as best it could
With the slow smokeless burning of decay.   40

Guiding Questions

Lines 1-9:

1. What is it about the landscape through which the speaker trudged that made it so disorientating? For what is the "frozen swamp" is a symbol (a psychological state, way of live, etc.)? What parallels do you see with the poem "Into My Own"?

Lines 10-22:

2. What error does the speaker suppose the fleeing bird to have made? How might the bird have discovered its error? How is the speaker making exactly the same error?

Lines 23-34

3. What is it about the wood-pile that draws the speaker's attention away from the bird? Note: "A cord is the amount of wood that, when 'racked and well stowed' (arranged so pieces are aligned, parallel, touching and compact), occupies a volume of 128 cubic feet (3.62 m³). This corresponds to a well-stacked woodpile 4 feet (122 cm) high, 8 feet (244 cm) wide, and 4 feet (122 cm) deep; or any other arrangement of linear measurements that yields the same volume" (Wikipedia contributors. "Cord (unit)").

Lines 34-40

5. What kind of person does the speaker imagine based on the wood-pile he constructed and left?

6. How does the author slow down the rhythm of the final line? Why?

Holistic:

7. There is no discernible rhyme scheme. However, the first and last lines do rhyme. Why?

Final Thoughts

The speaker is lost in a "frozen swamp," perhaps a metaphor for a suicidal frame of mind. Faced with the prospect of danger and disorientation, he is tempted to turn back to the safety of the known world of home, but he decides (rather too quickly and easily) to press on. (Compare "Into My Own.") He follows a bird and is "so foolish as to think what he [the bird] thought." This is the old error of anthropomorphizing animals that characters often make in Frost's poems. The man makes this mistake in thinking that the bird is leading him, but the bird makes the same mistake in thinking that the man is trying to get the white feather in its tail. In fact, the bird leads the man to the wood-pile quite by chance – our introduction to the arbitrary world of the poem.

The speaker examines the wood-pile from every angle trying to make sense of its presence. There is plenty of evidence: it is a precisely stacked cord of maple wood; it is the only such pile visible; there are no sled tracks to indicate how the wood was transported; it has evidently been there several years; and it has been carefully built against a growing tree and secured by a stake. All of this points to the conclusion that "Someone who lived in turning to fresh tasks" made the pile and then forgot about it, so the wood will never heat a house in "a useful fireplace." (Once again, we see the speaker's need to explain everything.) It simply remains slowly disintegrating. However, the "slow smokeless burning of decay" does in a way "warm the frozen swamp" for the decay of vegetable matter over millennia will turn the swamp into a fertile plain. This truth is the antithesis of both the man and the bird taking "Everything said as personal to himself."

Nature is impersonal. I am reminded of the conclusion of Camus' existentialist, or absurdist, novel *The Stranger* (1942) in which the protagonist, Meursault, finally has an epiphany, "… for the first time, in that night alive with signs and stars, I opened myself to the gentle indifference of the world." The wood-pile, so precisely made, may represent Frost's own poems. (At the time of writing [February, 1912], his poetry remained unpublished). The abandoned wood-pile is not a symbol of futility. In terms of writing, the poem asserts that even an unpublished poem is a thing of value to a reader who may, decades later, stumble across it and be moved by it.

Mountain Interval (1916)

Frost's American publisher Henry Holt and Company was anxious for a third collection to build upon the success of the first two and the result was *Mountain Interval* (late 1916). The collection was well reviewed, but sales were disappointing. Frost's biographer, Lawrance Thompson, established that twelve of the poems went back to before 1911, seven had been written in England and thirteen in the months since Frost's return to the States. This explains why the collection lacks the coherence and careful structure of Frost's first two books, although once again Frost printed the first and last poems ("The Road Not Taken" and "The Sound of Trees") in italics as prologue and afterward to the collection.

The title has a double meaning. 'Mountain interval' is a New England term for a valley between two peaks (Kendall 177). In his dedication to his wife, Frost referred to three intervals in their lives: "South Branch [farm in Franconia, New Hampshire] under black mountains ...the upper at Plymouth [New Hampshire] ... [and] the first interval of all ... the old farm [Hyla Brook in Derry, New Hampshire], our brook interval."

The Road Not Taken

Pre-reading

We have to make choices all the time. Most of them are trivial and have no long-term consequences (e.g., to drink coffee or tea; to watch one film or another; to go to the gym or skip today; etc.). However, we all make some decisions that we know in advance will probably affect the entire direction of our lives in ways we cannot precisely predict and will not be able to change because life has no do-overs (e.g., which college to attend; to begin, or to end, a relationship; taking one job offer and rejecting another; etc.).

Think of some of the life-changing decisions you have already made. What were the pros and cons of each choice? Why did you make the choices that you did? Looking back on your decision now, how do you feel about them? Any regrets?

What life-changing decisions are you going to have to make in the next ten years? How do you feel about the challenge that they pose?

From the first time he shared the poem with his friend Edward Thomas, Frost felt that readers had entirely misunderstood its point. Does any writer have the right to feel this way?

Listen to the song "Two Different Roads" by Michael Nesmith on Youtube. Nesmith deals with a similar theme.

TWO roads diverged in a yellow wood,
And sorry I could not travel both
And be one traveler, long I stood
And looked down one as far as I could
To where it bent in the undergrowth;   5

Then took the other, as just as fair,
And having perhaps the better claim,
Because it was grassy and wanted wear;
Though as for that the passing there
Had worn them really about the same,   10

And both that morning equally lay
In leaves no step had trodden black.
Oh, I kept the first for another day!
Yet knowing how way leads on to way,
I doubted if I should ever come back.   15

I shall be telling this with a sigh
Somewhere ages and ages hence:
Two roads diverged in a wood, and I –
I took the one less traveled by,
And that has made all the difference.   20

Guiding Questions

1. The poem is an extended metaphor. It really helps to visualize what is described, so create a diagram or map of the situation and annotate it with quotations and comments of your own.

Stanza One:

2. After making a binary choice (either this *or* that) why can you no longer be "one traveler"?

3. What limitation in decision-making is symbolized by the metaphorical bending of the road "in the undergrowth"?

4. Line 1 has two surprising words: "roads" and "yellow." You do not get "roads" in a wood: you get 'paths,' 'trails,' or 'ways'. Similarly, "yellow" is not the first color one associates with a wood: 'brown,' 'green' or 'budding' seem more appropriate. How does the writer's word choice affect your understanding of the poem?

Stanza Two:

5. What reason does the speaker give for, at the time, choosing one road over the other? How valid was this reason in retrospect? Do you think that the speaker knew these things about his decision-making at the time or only with the wisdom of hindsight? Explain your answer.

Stanza Three:

6. The phrase "trodden black" includes two very strong words (as compared, for example, with 'worn bare' or 'turned brown'). What is the effect of the poet's choice of words?

7. Explain why a person is unlikely ever to come back to a fork in the road whether it is a real one in a wood or a symbolic one in life.

Stanza Four:

8. How does the speaker know he will "be telling this with a sigh" a long time into his future?

9. What emotion do you think will be behind the speaker's "sigh" (Clue: Merriam-Webster defines 'sigh' as: "to take a deep audible breath [as in weariness or relief]." In sighing, Collins says: "you let out a deep breath, as a way of expressing feelings such as disappointment, tiredness, or pleasure." So a sigh may reflect *either* positive or negative feelings.)

10. Andrew Spacey gives this biographical background, "Robert Frost wrote this poem to highlight a trait of, and poke fun at, his friend Edward Thomas, an English-Welsh poet, who, when out walking with Frost in England would often regret not having taken a different path. Thomas would sigh over what they might have seen and done, and Frost thought this

quaintly romantic" (*Owlcation*). How does this information affect your view of the poem?

Holistic:

13. The poem has four stanzas of five lines (quintrains) with the rhyme scheme ABAAB. Each line has four stressed syllables though the pattern of stressed/unstressed syllables varies. How does the form of the poem contribute to your experience in reading it? Consider particularly the impact of run-on lines.

Final Thoughts

The ambiguity of this poem is rooted in the controversial debate about free will versus determinism: humans believe that they make choices freely, but those choices are actually circumscribed and even controlled by forces beyond our control of which we may be unconscious (cultural and religious norms and values, our parenting and education, the way in which certain behaviors are 'hard-wired' in the brain, etc.)

That's a response that takes the poem seriously. Interpreting it as intentionally comic, one can point to the pompous solemnity of the speaker's tone. Constantly asking, "What if..." (although perhaps inevitable and all-too-human) is completely pointless. Looking backward prevents a person from living in the moment and moving into the future, and a person who does this all the time deserves to be laughed at.

Birches

Pre-reading

The idea of climbing a birch tree to near the top, then flinging one's legs out so that the flexible trunk of the tree bends (something like the pole used in pole vaulting) and riding it down until one can let go near to the ground might seem a little hair-raising, but it cannot have been as dangerous as it sounds because Frost's daughter Lesley recorded in her journal, "On the way home, i climbed up a high birch and came down with it and i stopped in the air about three feet and pap cout me" (sic).

Were you ever a climber (of furniture, trees, rocks, climbing walls, etc.)? What was the attraction? What did it feel like?

When I see birches bend to left and right
Across the lines of straighter darker trees,
I like to think some boy's been swinging them.
But swinging doesn't bend them down to stay
As ice-storms do. Often you must have seen them   5
Loaded with ice a sunny winter morning
After a rain. They click upon themselves
As the breeze rises, and turn many-colored
As the stir cracks and crazes their enamel.
Soon the sun's warmth makes them shed crystal shells   10
Shattering and avalanching on the snow-crust –
Such heaps of broken glass to sweep away
You'd think the inner dome of heaven had fallen.
They are dragged to the withered bracken by the load,
And they seem not to break; though once they are bowed   15
So low for long, they never right themselves:
You may see their trunks arching in the woods
Years afterwards, trailing their leaves on the ground
Like girls on hands and knees that throw their hair
Before them over their heads to dry in the sun.   20
But I was going to say when Truth broke in
With all her matter-of-fact about the ice-storm
I should prefer to have some boy bend them
As he went out and in to fetch the cows –

Some boy too far from town to learn baseball,   25
Whose only play was what he found himself,
Summer or winter, and could play alone.
One by one he subdued his father's trees
By riding them down over and over again
Until he took the stiffness out of them,   30
And not one but hung limp, not one was left
For him to conquer. He learned all there was
To learn about not launching out too soon
And so not carrying the tree away
Clear to the ground. He always kept his poise   35
To the top branches, climbing carefully
With the same pains you use to fill a cup
Up to the brim, and even above the brim.
Then he flung outward, feet first, with a swish,
Kicking his way down through the air to the ground.   40
So was I once myself a swinger of birches.
And so I dream of going back to be.
It's when I'm weary of considerations,
And life is too much like a pathless wood
Where your face burns and tickles with the cobwebs   45
Broken across it, and one eye is weeping
From a twig's having lashed across it open.
I'd like to get away from earth awhile
And then come back to it and begin over.
May no fate willfully misunderstand me   50
And half grant what I wish and snatch me away
Not to return. Earth's the right place for love:
I don't know where it's likely to go better.
I'd like to go by climbing a birch tree,
And climb black branches up a snow-white trunk   55
Toward heaven, till the tree could bear no more,
But dipped its top and set me down again.
That would be good both going and coming back.
One could do worse than be a swinger of birches.

Guiding Questions

This poem was partly inspired by another poem, "Swinging on a Birch-tree" by American poet Lucy Larcom (see Appendix 1), and partly by Frost's own experience of swinging on birch trees in his childhood. Frost is reported to have said, "[I]t was almost sacrilegious climbing a birch tree till it bent, till it gave and swooped to the ground, but that's what boys did in those days" (Wikipedia contributors. "Birches [poem]").

Lines 1-20

1. The speaker considers two reasons why birch trees might be permanently bent. What are they? Why does he dismiss his first idea? Why does he still prefer this idea to the second which he finally has to accept?

2. In lines 7 to 13, how does the poet capture the sight and the sound as the build-up of ice on the bark of a birch tree melts and fractures in the winter sun? Consider the use of metaphors ("cracks and crazes their enamel … shed crystal shells … avalanching on the snow-crust … heaps of broken glass to sweep away … the inner dome of heaven had fallen") and the way alliteration and assonance are used to convey the sound of the cracking ice.

3. Winter ice does permanent damage to the birches which stay bent; they never recover. What does this suggest about the nature of existence whether it is for flora, fauna or human?

4. The final description of the bent birches is a simile, "trailing their leaves on the ground / Like girls on hands and knees that throw their hair / Before them over their heads to dry in the sun." What do you make of that comparison? Some critics have suggested that there is a strong erotic suggestion in the description of the boy climbing the birch trees and coming back down. Do you agree?

Lines 21-40

5. On lines 21 and 23 we learn that the speaker has made a false start: ice-damage to birches is not his topic, swinging on birch trees is. What contrast and opposition do these three lines establish? Why do you think that the word "Truth" is capitalized?

6. What is significant about the kind of boy the speaker imagines to have bent the trees? (Clue: The word "alone" seems to me the single most important word in the description.)

7. The words "subdued" and "conquer" are very strong verbs. They suggest a symbolic significance to the mastering of birch trees. What do you think the speaker has in mind?

8. Why is it important to avoid "launching out too soon" when swinging

down on a birch tree? What is going to happen if you do that?

9. To describe the imagined boy's skill, the speaker uses a simile on lines 37-38. How effective is this comparison in communicating the skill needed?

10. Comment on the onomatopoeia in line 39.

Lines 41-54

11. Nostalgia enters the poem: the speaker is an adult now but thinks fondly of regaining the freedom to climb birch trees and swing back down to earth that he had as a boy. What do you think he means when he says he wants to do this most when he is "weary of considerations"? What connection, if any, do you see between the bending of birches by ice and the difficulties that the speaker faces as an adult?

12. Lines 44 to 47 use an extended metaphor to describe the frustrations of adult life. Comment on the effectiveness of the comparisons. The word "across" is repeated. Why?

13. Why does the speaker want "to get away from earth awhile / And then come back to it and begin over"? What might climbing, "*Toward* heaven" symbolize?

14. Why does he certainly not want to die? What would be the ideal for him?

Holistic:

15. The poem is written in blank verse with flexibility in the iambic pentameter. Alliteration, assonance, caesura and enjambment are used in the poem. Comment on any examples you find particularly effective.

Final Thoughts

Frost called "Birches" (originally "Swinging Birches") "two fragments soldered together," one on the ice-storm bending birch trees down and the other on the experience of swinging them down (respectively the "Truth" of rational thought and the truth of imagination). This raises an important question as to how well these two parts fit together into a coherent whole.

What for the boy is merely a form of play is for the man a transcendent escape from the heavy Truth of the earthly plane of existence. The Truth of life in the real world, whether that be the life of nature (flora and fauna) or of society (humanity), is placed in opposition or contrast to the world of fantasy and imagination. The ultimate escape from earth (the world of reality) would, of course, be death, ascending up into whatever heaven the speaker conceives of and not coming back. However, this is definitely not what he wants. Instead, he desires only a respite from the struggles of the earthly level so that he can return refreshed and reinvigorated to continue striving for love on earth. Life on earth may be imperfect, but it is the only life we have.

Climbing a birch tree is a perfect metaphor for what it is that the speaker longs. The birch tree is rooted in the soil, so by climbing it one still has some connection with the earth, and one chooses one's own moment to return to the ground by skillfully thrusting out one's legs. The paths up and down are "good both going and coming back." I think it is productive to see the basic contrast in the poem in terms of literary imagination on the one hand and living rationally in the real world on the other. Frost needed to escape into the heightened, idealized world of the poetry, but not at the expense of his obligations as husband, father, farmer, neighbor, etc. By the end of the poem a balance has been achieved between the world of the imagination and the world of commonsense reality, both of which we all inhabit. Read this way, the poem has coherence.

A Time to Talk

Pre-reading

The story goes that the English Romantic poet Samuel Taylor Coleridge (1772-1834) had an opium-influenced dream after reading a book describing Xanadu, the summer palace of the Mongol ruler and Emperor of China, Kublai Khan. When he woke up he felt that he had in his head the plan for an entire poem in excess of two hundred lines, and he began writing. Having got to line 54, "a person from Porlock" knocked on his door and paid the poet a social call. When the unidentified man had gone, Coleridge found that he could not complete the poem because the interruption had caused him to forget the remaining lines.

Ever been interrupted by the unexpected (even unwelcome) appearance of a friend when you were doing something on which you really wanted to concentrate? What did you do? How did you feel?

WHEN a friend calls to me from the road
And slows his horse to a meaning walk,
I don't stand still and look around
On all the hills I haven't hoed,
And shout from where I am, What is it?   5
No, not as there is a time to talk.
I thrust my hoe in the mellow ground,
Blade-end up and five feet tall,
And plod: I go up to the stone wall
For a friendly visit.   10

Guiding Questions

1. What farming activity is the speaker engaged in and what good reason does he have for wanting (even needing) to get on with it?

2. How does he react when a friend calls to him? How does he feel about having to stop his task?

3. What is meant by the phrase "a meaning walk"?

4. Comment on the heavy alliteration on the letters: 's' in line 3; 'h' in line 4; 'n' and 't' in line 6; and 'f' in line 8. What effect is produced in each case?

5. Why would the speaker have to "plod" to the wall? Why did the poet not just use the word "walk"?

6. Why do you think that he calls the ground "mellow"? What relationship does it suggest that the speaker has with his land? (Clue: Merriam-Webster defines "mellow" as "pleasantly rich, full, or soft.")

7. The description of the hoe thrust into the ground, "Blade-end up and five feet tall," creates a strong visual image. What does this image communicate to you as reader?

8. Thinking back to the poem "Mending Wall" what do you make of the description of the speaker going "up to" but not over "the stone wall / For a friendly visit."

9. The poem rhymes: ABCADBCEED. What does rhyme contribute to the experience of reading the poem?

Final Thoughts

A hoe is a long-handled implement with a thin, flat blade that is used to slice into the ground cutting and destroying the roots of weeds growing around and among a crop. It's a pretty laborious activity, but it is essential to getting a good yield from whatever crop has been planted (at least it was before the use of chemical weed killers). Now, working the land is a common theme in Frost's poetry, as is the sense of satisfaction that a person gets from making the earth productive. Friendship is, however, an even higher value in Frost's poems where people often feel isolated from their fellow humans. That is why friendship needs to be nurtured. The hoeing can always be done later, but the chance to talk to a friend is an opportunity that has to be grasped before it is lost. Life is too short and too uncertain to pass up the change of a chat with a friend – the chance might never come again.

Interestingly, this seems to be a case where, "'Good fences make good neighbors.'" Neither man intrudes into the other's space. The friend apparently stays on the road and does not dismount his horse; the speaker stays on his side of the wall, that is, on ground that belongs to him. Both men know the exact terms of their friendship which means that they do not have to waste time rediscovering or reestablishing the boundaries. They can just talk.

The Hill Wife

Pre-reading
Ever felt that another person just does not understand your feelings?

LONELINESS

(Her Word)
ONE ought not to have to care
  So much as you and I
Care when the birds come round the house
  To seem to say good-bye;

Or care so much when they come back   5
  With whatever it is they sing;
The truth being we are as much
  Too glad for the one thing

As we are too sad for the other here–
  With birds that fill their breasts   10
But with each other and themselves
  And their built or driven nests.

HOUSE FEAR

Always – I tell you this they learned –
Always at night when they returned
To the lonely house from far away   15
To lamps unlighted and fire gone gray,
They learned to rattle the lock and key
To give whatever might chance to be
Warning and time to be off in flight:
And preferring the out- to the in-door night,   20
They learned to leave the house-door wide
Until they had lit the lamp inside.

THE SMILE

(Her Word)
I didn't like the way he went away.
That smile! It never came of being gay.
Still he smiled – did you see him? – I was sure!   25
Perhaps because we gave him only bread
And the wretch knew from that that we were poor.
Perhaps because he let us give instead
Of seizing from us as he might have seized.
Perhaps he mocked at us for being wed,   30
Or being very young (and he was pleased
To have a vision of us old and dead).
I wonder how far down the road he's got.
He's watching from the woods as like as not.

THE OFT-REPEATED DREAM

She had no saying dark enough   35
  For the dark pine that kept
Forever trying the window-latch
  Of the room where they slept.

The tireless but ineffectual hands
  That with every futile pass   40
Made the great tree seem as a little bird
  Before the mystery of glass!

It never had been inside the room,
  And only one of the two
Was afraid in an oft-repeated dream   45
  Of what the tree might do.

THE IMPULSE

It was too lonely for her there,
  And too wild,
And since there were but two of them,
  And no child,   50

And work was little in the house,
  She was free,
And followed where he furrowed field,
  Or felled tree.

She rested on a log and tossed   55
  The fresh chips,
With a song only to herself
  On her lips.

And once she went to break a bough
  Of black alder.   60
She strayed so far she scarcely heard
  When he called her –

And didn't answer – didn't speak –
  Or return.
She stood, and then she ran and hid   65
  In the fern.

He never found her, though he looked
  Everywhere,
And he asked at her mother's house
  Was she there.   70

Sudden and swift and light as that
  The ties gave,
And he learned of finalities
  Besides the grave.

Study Guide

Guiding Questions

Loneliness:

The voice is that of a farmer's wife.

1. Why does she think that she and her husband "have" to care about the movements of the birds?

2. What mistake does the speaker think that she and her husband are making in being, "Too glad for the one thing ... [and] too sad for the other"?

3. In what ways does she think that the birds are very different in their concerns from her husband and herself?

4. Note: "[D]riven nests" appears to mean: nests that are not yet finished but which the birds feel driven by instinct to build. Look carefully at lines 10 to 13. What differences between the birds and the married couple are implied?

House Fear:

The voice is that of a third person omniscient narrator who describes the habitual way in which the husband and wife entered their home when returning late at night.

5. What does the repetition of the word "Always" imply about the behavior of the two?

6. Is it really the house that is "lonely"? (Clue: look up the term 'transferred epithet.')

7. Similarly the description of the "lamps unlighted and fire gone gray" in the farmhouse seems to be a metaphor for the state of the couple's marriage. What does the metaphor tell us?

8. The couple seems to be making a noise so that any intruder (human or animal) can have time "to be off in flight." Metaphorically, what is it that the couple is trying to get rid of?

9. What reason do the man and wife give themselves why they prefer to stay outside and leave the door open until they have lit a light in the house? What do you think that the "in-door night" represents (symbolizes)?

The Smile:

The voice of the wife describes her feelings about a hobo (tramp) who has come up to the farm looking for a handout.

10. There is something paranoid about the woman's reaction to the smile of the hobo. After all, a smile is normally a friendly, benevolent facial expression. In lines 23 to 27, how does she explain the man's smile to her own satisfaction? Is there a simpler explanation than hers?

93

11. What further rationalization does she come up with in lines 28-29?

12. What further rationalization does she come up with in lines 30-32?

13. Do you notice any trend or progression in her explanations? Comment on the effect of the repetition of the word "Perhaps."

14. The rhyming of the words "wed" and "dead" is particularly forceful. What is suggested by the poet about the woman's deepest thoughts by making her link these two words?

15. When she "wonder[s] how far down the road he's got," there is a new element in her feelings about the man. I would identify it as envy. What about the man's life might the woman envy?

16. What is her last paranoid fear?

The Oft-Repeated Dream:
Back to the voice of a third person omniscient narrator.

17. Analyze the extended personification of the pine tree. How does the woman's description make it sound threatening? (Comment on the repetition of the word "dark.")

18. Why is glass a "mystery" to a bird?

19. The sound of the tree against the window panes obviously penetrates into the woman's unconscious while she is asleep and reappears in an "oft-repeated" nightmare. Why is it significant that "only one of the two" has this nightmare?

The Impulse:
Staying with the voice of a third person omniscient narrator.

20. Comment on the irony that the wife finds the farmhouse "too lonely for her there, / And too wild."

21. Comment on the irony of the narrator's judgment "She was free."

22. Notice the repetition of the word "too." What does it show about the wife's state of mind?

23. The rhyme of "free" and "tree" is particularly strong. How might a tree be associated in the woman's mind with freedom?

24. In lines 51 to 54, there are only three verbs describing the actions of the woman and her husband: "followed," "furrowed" and "felled." Contrast the first of these with the other two. What does the contrast show of the different life-experience of the woman and the man?

25. In stanza three, the wife does not appear to act like a human at all but rather an animal. Any suggestions?

26. Comment on the alliteration of the letters 'b' and 's' in lines 59 to 61.

27. The word "strayed" seems to be carefully chosen for its connotations.

In what senses is the woman straying?

28. How does the rhythm of lines 63-64 convey that the woman acts on impulse?

29. Why is the single word "Everywhere" so effective?

30. Some critics see the woman as having been transformed into a bird that flies away to freedom. What support for this interpretation do you find in these lines?

31. The narrator says "The ties gave." What do you understand by the "ties" in this context?

32. Note: The word "Besides" means 'other than.' What finalities other than death do you think that the loss of his wife taught the man?

Holistic:

33. In what different senses is the woman a "Hill Wife" at the start of the poem and at its end?

Final Thoughts:

Writing in 1957, the critic Yvor Winters said of this poem, "The poem has an eerie quality, like that of dream or of neurosis, but it has little else. As a study in human relationships, it amounts to nothing … if serious steps are to be lightly taken, then poetry, at least, is impoverished, and the poet can have very little to say" (*The Function of Criticism*). This may not be Frost's greatest poem, but it is more profound than Winters suggests.

"The Hill Wife" and "The Smile" are identified as "Her word." In the other three poems, the voice is that of the third person omniscient narrator. The husband's voice is never heard. It seems that the poet warns us not to accept the wife's words uncritically. Her perspective quickly emerges as very biased; she is an unreliable and perhaps unhinged narrator.

"The Hill Wife" tells the story of a farmer and his wife who are trapped in a vicious cycle which ultimately destroys their marriage. On the one hand, the reader sees the woman's deepening psychosis, and on the other the repeated failure of the man to understand her fears, to empathize with them, or to offer the emotional support that she so desperately seeks and needs.

In "Loneliness" the woman tries to share with her husband her sense that something must be wrong with them to be so emotionally invested in the comings and goings of the birds around their house, to invest with human significance behavior that is simply natural. The problem is that the women cannot put into words the emptiness she is feeling, it comes out only by implication: the fiction that the birds are in some sort of relationship with the couple points to the fact that the man and woman are not in a relationship with each other; the singing of the birds highlights the couple's own silence; the nest-building of the birds is in contrast to the childless farmhouse. Perhaps the woman senses that the birds have become surrogate children.

"House Fear" shows the fear that the man and woman have of entering their own house and the elaborate precautions they take in doing so. The house is defined by absence: no life, no light, no warmth, which together symbolize the failing marriage of the man and wife. It is they who seem to be the intruders; it is they who fear entering the house together because of the emptiness of their relationship.

The woman's reaction to the tramp in "The Smile" is evidently paranoid since he appears to be both grateful and friendly: she sees a threat where none exists. However, though she fears this man, the woman also envies his ability to walk away, and it is perhaps here that she gets the idea that she too can escape "far down the road."

"The Oft-Repeated Dream" details a confused nightmare that troubles the wife, but only the wife, "only one of the two." The tree outside their bedroom window is sometimes a dark, nameless human or animal intruder trying to open the locked window and sometimes a little bird scratching on the pane bewildered by "the mystery of glass." Thus, it is both powerful and terrifying, and helpless and pitiable. It is unclear what the tree in the nightmare represents – as symbols often are unclear in dreams. Sigmund Freud might have found it a sexual figure, representing the woman's fear of her husband's sexual advances, or perhaps a repressed memory of being sexually abused as a child. In contrast, it may represent some force of nature trying to free her from the artificial confinement of the house and the marriage that is stifling her. Birds throughout the poem appear to represent freedom. Perhaps the bird is trying to set her free. The power of the symbolism lies in its very ambiguity.

In "The Impulse" the wife follows her silent husband into field and wood, hoping that his nearness might relieve her fear of loneliness. Without a child to care for and with little to do around the house, the woman is "free" – ironically, she is free to obsess over her confinement. Unlike the woman, the man is fully occupied with manual labor (compare "Home Burial"). He gives his attention to plowing and cutting down trees – no time for self-reflection, no time to show love and concern for his wife. The description in stanza three certainly makes the woman appear like a bird sitting on the log, tossing up the wood chips and singing to herself. Note the contrast with "Loneliness" where the woman sought to communicate with her husband. Now she seems to have given up on that.

The "bough / Of black alder" that she goes to "break" symbolizes her relationship with her husband, their marriage, and the vow (rhymes with "bough") that she made to love, honor and obey him. She wonders off into the wood, "so far she scarcely heard / When he called her," symbolizing the emotional distance that has grown between the two. Having failed for so long to communicate with his wife, she no longer wants to hear anything that he has to say; she no longer recognizes that he has any claim upon her. She becomes the wife of the hill by hiding in the fern. The woman disappears into the world of nature never to be seen again.

Ironically, when it is too late, the man shows the love and concern for his wife that he so evidently failed to show when they were together. The rhythm and diction of stanza six leave the reader in no doubt that the husband desperately wants to find his wife and exerts himself to the fullest to do so. It is this that adds to his tragedy, for he has realized too late just what he has lost. He is that common figure in Frost's poetry, the victim of just how instantly life can change, "Sudden and swift and light as that / The ties gave," yet unlike, for example, the boy in "'Out, out–,'" he is culpable. Ironically, at the end of the poem it is the man who is left isolated and lonely having "learned of finalities / Besides the grave," for he has lost the thing he loved (but was not conscious of loving) just as finally as if she had died.

The Exposed Nest

Pre-reading

Ever found an injured or helpless animal (particularly a young one) and tried
to help it? What motivated you to do that? What practical action were you
able to take? How did things work out? How did that make you feel?

Ever shared a memory with someone long after the experience you had with
them? How did it go? Did they have the same memories you had? The same
feelings?

YOU were forever finding some new play.
So when I saw you down on hands and knees
In the meadow, busy with the new-cut hay,
Trying, I thought, to set it up on end,
I went to show you how to make it stay,   5
If that was your idea, against the breeze,
And, if you asked me, even help pretend
To make it root again and grow afresh.
But 'twas no make-believe with you to-day,
Nor was the grass itself your real concern,   10
Though I found your hand full of wilted fern,
Steel-bright June-grass, and blackening heads of clover.
'Twas a nest full of young birds on the ground
The cutter-bar had just gone champing over
(Miraculously without tasting flesh)   15
And left defenseless to the heat and light.
You wanted to restore them to their right
Of something interposed between their sight
And too much world at once – could means be found.
The way the nest-full every time we stirred   20
Stood up to us as to a mother-bird
Whose coming home has been too long deferred,
Made me ask would the mother-bird return
And care for them in such a change of scene
And might our meddling make her more afraid.   25

That was a thing we could not wait to learn.
We saw the risk we took in doing good,
But dared not spare to do the best we could
Though harm should come of it; so built the screen
You had begun, and gave them back their shade.   30
All this to prove we cared. Why is there then
No more to tell? We turned to other things.
I haven't any memory – have you? –
Of ever coming to the place again
To see if the birds lived the first night through,   35
And so at last to learn to use their wings.

Guiding Questions

1. This is a dramatic monologue with the speaker talking to someone about a shared past experience. Who are these two and what do you learn about their relationship?

Lines 1-8:

2. The tone of the first eight lines is playful, but there is a more serious undertone. What did the speaker assume about the other's activity? What skill did he feel he could offer to help the other? The speaker says he was willing "if you asked me, even help pretend / To make [the grass] root again and grow afresh." How does the word "pretend" emphasize the speaker's limitations?

Lines 9-25:

3. Describe the change of tone that you perceive at line 9. How is this change achieved?

4. Analyze the personification of the mowing machine. How does it introduce the theme of death?

5. What is meant by saying the birds had been exposed to "so much world at once"? How does the description of the birds stress their innocence and vulnerability?

Lines 26-36

6. On lines 26-27, the speaker changes his pronouns from singular ("I ... you") to plural ('we"). Comment on the significance of this change.

7. Explain how the line, "We saw the risk we took in doing good," captures the dilemma of the two as they tried to save the baby birds. Why does the speaker now call what they did "meddling"? Exactly what harm could come of their intervention?

8. Having done "the best" they could, the speaker recalls that they then "turned to other things." How does the speaker judge their moving on with their lives and forgetting all about the birds? How do you as reader judge that action? Is there a difference? Why / why not?

9. Why do you think that the speaker asks the other person if he/she has any memory of them both ever returning to check up on the birds?

Holistic:

10. The speaker really seems to understand the thoughts and feelings of young children without being condescending or patronizing. Give and comment on some examples of this.

11. In what ways does the rhythm and rhyme of lines 27-36 differ from that of lines 1-26? What causes that difference? (Note: The poem has a very complex, irregular rhyme scheme: ABACAB CDAEEFGFDHHHGIIIEJKELLJKMNOPOQ.)

Final Thoughts

This is a poem about human fallibility. Children go through a phase where they think that their father and mother can answer every question and solve every problem. The speaker here is honest enough to admit in retrospect to himself and to his child that he was never this super-parent. However, the honesty with which he speaks, and the evident regret that he feels, does win him the reader's respect. Life can be very cruel, and it is not always possible, despite the best intentions of our wish to do so, to 'make things better.'

Critics frequently make the point that "The Exposed Nest" was published in 1916, two years into World War I (1914-1918) at a time when England was facing the terrible loss of young, innocent lives on the Western Front. It is argued that Frost had that in mind in this poem. We know, however, that many of the poems Frost included in his early books had been written years previously while he was still farming in New Hampshire. I should not, therefore, want to ascribe intention to the poet, but we also know that the implications of Frost's poems go well beyond the limits of their ostensible setting, plot and themes.

"Out, out –"

Pre-reading

Unusually, Frost uses a quotation as the title of a poem. The words come from Shakespeare's play *Macbeth*. The eponymous hero, who has just heard about the death of his wife, says: "Out, out, brief candle! / Life's but a walking shadow, a poor player, / That struts and frets his hour upon the stage, / And then is heard no more" (5.5). How do you feel about this bleak, existential view of the nature of human life?

Most of us have personally witnessed a tragic accident or its immediate aftermath (particularly tragic when the victim is a child), and we have all seen reports on the media. If you can, share your experience in discussion. If not, think upon it. Reflect on your feelings.

THE BUZZ-SAW snarled and rattled in the yard
And made dust and dropped stove-length sticks of wood,
Sweet-scented stuff when the breeze drew across it.
And from there those that lifted eyes could count
Five mountain ranges one behind the other   5
Under the sunset far into Vermont.
And the saw snarled and rattled, snarled and rattled,
As it ran light, or had to bear a load.
And nothing happened: day was all but done.
Call it a day, I wish they might have said   10
To please the boy by giving him the half hour
That a boy counts so much when saved from work.
His sister stood beside them in her apron
To tell them "Supper." At the word, the saw,
As if to prove saws knew what supper meant,   15
Leaped out at the boy's hand, or seemed to leap –
He must have given the hand. However it was,

102

Neither refused the meeting. But the hand!
The boy's first outcry was a rueful laugh,
As he swung toward them holding up the hand   20
Half in appeal, but half as if to keep
The life from spilling. Then the boy saw all –
Since he was old enough to know, big boy
Doing a man's work, though a child at heart –
He saw all spoiled. "Don't let him cut my hand off –   25
The doctor, when he comes. Don't let him, sister!"
So. But the hand was gone already.
The doctor put him in the dark of ether.
He lay and puffed his lips out with his breath.
And then – the watcher at his pulse took fright.   30
No one believed. They listened at his heart.
Little – less – nothing! – and that ended it.
No more to build on there. And they, since they
Were not the one dead, turned to their affairs.

Guiding Questions

Lines 1-9:

1. The opening of the poem is full of contrasts. Identify them. How does the description of the setting stress its beauty? What are the ominous undertones in the description?

2. Look carefully at these words, "THE BUZZ-SAW ... those that lifted eyes." What do they foreshadow? (Clue: The saw produces "dust." Compare, "dust thou art, and unto dust shalt thou return" (*Genesis* 3.19, *KJV*).

3. Comment on how the personification of the saw that begins on the first line is developed.

4. Analyze the use of caesura and alliteration on line 9.

Lines 10-18:

5. How is the personification of the saw further developed here?

6. Examine the rhythm of lines 14 to 18. How is it different from the rhythm of the lines up to this point? How is that difference achieved by the writer? What effect does this change have?

7. "But the hand!" is an incomplete exclamation. What do you think the speaker is trying to say?

Lines 19-27:

8. What is characteristically child-like about the boy's reaction to the accident?

9. The description "big boy" is an oxymoron. How and why does the speaker stress the ambiguity of the boy's age and his role on the farm?

10. Comment on the repetition of the pun on "saw" in line 22 and line 25: "Then the boy saw all –" and "He saw all spoiled." Is this supposed to be comic? Is the pun deliberate?

11. What is particularly pathetic about the boy's plea to his sister?

Lines 28-34:

12. How does the rhythm of these lines capture the rapidly changing nature of the situation and of the feelings of those who witnessed it?

13. The speaker states simply, "that ended it." However, this is also an ambiguous statement. What is the "it" that ended? (Clue: There is more than one answer to this question.)

14. What justification does the speaker suggest for the reaction of the other farm workers in turning "to their [own] affairs" and getting on with their lives? How do you as reader react to their reaction? (Note: There is an obvious parallel with "The Exposed Nest.")

Holistic:
15. The poem is written in blank verse, but only lines 1, 9, 14, 15, 19, 22, 29 and 33 are in regular iambic pentameter. Frequent use is made of caesura, enjambment, repetition, alliteration and assonance. Comment on any of these features that contribute to your reading experience.

Final Thoughts

Like many of Frost's poems, this is autobiographical: Frost's New Hampshire acquaintance Raymond Tracy Fitzgerald (aged 16) died on March 24th, 1910, in an accident similar to that in the poem. Given its publication date (July 1916) some argue that "the poem can be read as a critique as to how warfare can force innocent, young boys to leave their childhood behind, and ultimately be destroyed by circumstances created by the 'responsible' adult" (Wikipedia contributors. "Out, Out –"). Such a reading is possible, even if Frost did not intend it. Life is fragile: it can be snuffed out very easily.

Chance plays a massive role in our lives. Several times the poem raises the sad thought, 'If only….' If only they had not been working so late … If only the boy had been told to stop early … If only the sister had not distracted him by calling "Supper!" … and so on. Either way, this boy's life is tragically ended too soon. Is it heartless for us to go on with our lives, go back to the things we *can* control or "build on"? Or is that the only possible reaction to tragedy? The poem only poses the question; the reader must answer it .....

New Hampshire (1923)

Introduction

Frost's fourth collection, published in November 1923, had the subtitle *A Poem with Notes and Grace Notes.* The collection (which would be Frost's biggest) was divided into two sections: the title poem, "Notes" containing thirteen poems and "Grace Notes" containing thirty poems. (Fagan tells us that this structure was Frost's comic parody of T. S. Eliot's "heavily footnoted ... *The Waste Land*," part of the joke being that Frost's footnotes refer to other poems by him in the same volume while Eliot's refer to a wide range of literary works [235].) It received excellent reviews, sold well, and earned Frost his first Pulitzer Prize.

The Census-Taker

Pre-reading

Ever been to the site of an abandoned house? (I remember going up to the high Yorkshire Moors in England on a freezing cold October day to see Top Withens, the ruined farmhouse that is supposed to have been the inspiration for Wuthering Heights in Emily Bronte's novel of that name.) What did it feel like to know that people had lived, loved, laughed, cried and died there without leaving much of a trace of their existence?

I came an errand one cloud-blowing evening
To a slab-built, black-paper-covered house
Of one room and one window and one door,
The only dwelling in a waste cut over
A hundred square miles round it in the mountains: 5
And that not dwelt in now by men or women
(It never had been dwelt in, though, by women,
So what is this I make a sorrow of?)
I came as census-taker to the waste
To count the people in it and found none,   10
None in the hundred miles, none in the house,

Where I came last with some hope, but not much
After hours' overlooking from the cliffs
An emptiness flayed to the very stone.
I found no people that dared show themselves,   15
None not in hiding from the outward eye.
The time was autumn, but how anyone
Could tell the time of year when every tree
That could have dropped a leaf was down itself
And nothing but the stump of it was left   20
Now bringing out its rings in sugar of pitch;
And every tree up stood a rotting trunk
Without a single leaf to spend on autumn,
Or branch to whistle after what was spent.
Perhaps the wind the more without the help   25
Of breathing trees said something of the time
Of year or day the way it swung a door
Forever off the latch, as if rude men
Passed in and slammed it shut each one behind him
For the next one to open for himself.   30
I counted nine I had no right to count
(But this was dreamy unofficial counting)
Before I made the tenth across the threshold.
Where was my supper? Where was anyone's?
No lamp was lit. Nothing was on the table.   35
The stove was cold – the stove was off the chimney—
And down by one side where it lacked a leg.
The people that had loudly passed the door
Were people to the ear but not the eye.
They were not on the table with their elbows.   40
They were not sleeping in the shelves of bunks.
I saw no men there and no bones of men there.
I armed myself against such bones as might be
With the pitch-blackened stub of an axe-handle
I picked up off the straw-dust covered floor.   45
Not bones, but the ill-fitted window rattled.
The door was still because I held it shut
While I thought what to do that could be done—
About the house – about the people not there.

107

This house in one year fallen to decay   50
Filled me with no less sorrow than the houses
Fallen to ruin in ten thousand years
Where Asia wedges Africa from Europe.
Nothing was left to do that I could see
Unless to find that there was no one there   55
And declare to the cliffs too far for echo
'The place is desert and let whoso lurks
In silence, if in this he is aggrieved,
Break silence now or be forever silent.
Let him say why it should not be declared so.'   60
The melancholy of having to count souls
Where they grow fewer and fewer every year
Is extreme where they shrink to none at all.
It must be I want life to go on living.

Guiding Questions

To take a census is to count the human population. Census-taking is an expression of man's ability to bring order out of chaos, of man's power of reason over the wildness of nature. In contrast, the "waste cut over / A hundred square miles" is evidence of man's capacity to exploit and destroy nature, robbing the land of what is profitable and then moving on to do the same somewhere else.

Lines 1-14:

1. The setting is stark and bare. How does the speaker establish the nature of the house that he approaches?

2. In what ways does the size of the house contrast with the size of the "waste cut over" that surrounds it? What point is the poet making by this contrast in scale?

3. Explain how this wasteland has been created. What does the speaker mean by calling it, "An emptiness flayed to the very stone"?

4. The speaker seems to go out of his way to comment that the house "never had been dwelt in … by women." Why do you think this is a significant detail? (Clue: Think about the presentation of gender differences in other

Frost poems.)
Lines 15-24
5. Why does the speaker feel that the people who once lived in the house would not dare to "show themselves"? Why would they naturally hide from a visitor?
6. What do you think he means when he says that these people are all "in hiding from the outward eye"? (Clue: What about the 'inward eye' with which the census-taker sees these people very clearly? Explain.)
7. What is the effect of the alliteration of the letter 't' on lines 17-18?
8. In his description of the surrounding waste, how does the speaker convey how unnatural it is? What emotions are conveyed by the description?
Lines 25-33:
9. The census-taker is reduced to counting the number of times the door swings shut. Why does he say, "I had no right to count"? How does he justify his act of counting the banging of the door?
Lines 34-46:
10. This section is dominated by negatives. The house or shack is defined by absence: absence of people, of the things that sustain life, and even of the evidence that people were once there. What does he mean when he says that the people who lived there were "people to the ear but not the eye"? Make a list of the words that describe sounds that he associates with these absent people. Why does he pick up a "pitch-blackened stub of an axe-handle" from the floor?
11. Comment on the deliberate (even humorous) anti-climax of the line, "Not bones, but the ill-fitted window rattled."
Lines 47-60:
12. As a census-taker, what problem does the empty house pose to the speaker? What does he finally decide is the appropriate reaction?
13. We learn that this particular house has "in one year fallen to decay." (Presumably this means that the census-taker knew it when there were men inhabiting it.) Explain why the speaker finds this ruin no less sorrowful than ruins from ancient times.
14. It seems a little weird that the speaker should feel the need to shout a sort of challenge to any humans hiding from his sight. Why exactly does he do this? Why is it important to him to confront the ghosts of the house's occupants with the truth that, "'The place is desert'"? Why might they be "'aggrieved'" by this accusation?

Lines 61-64:

15. The final four lines of the poem are somber. Finding that the human population has shrunk to "none at all" has a profoundly depressing impact on the speaker. A lot depends, however, on the reader's understanding of the last line, "It must be I want life to go on living." The word 'want' can mean either: 1. a lack or deficiency of something (a dearth, deprivation or need for), or 2. a desire for something (a wish, demand or longing). How do you understand this line?

Final Thoughts

This poem describes the very antithesis of the values of the New England farmers who appear so frequently in Frost's poems. These men, their wives and their families normally have a close, multi-generational connection with the land. It is true that, as in "Mowing" and "The Exposed Nest," farming involves some inevitable destruction (grasses have to be cut down for fodder, resulting in some loss of creatures' natural habitat), but this is at its best simply a part of the natural cycle of seeding, generation, birth, life and death. Ultimately, man is in harmony with nature. Here, however, man is motivated by quick profit simply to exploit nature with no thought to the consequences (which in this case would be not only ugliness but erosion of the hillsides).

Having said that, Frank Lentricchia has called this poem "as explicit a confrontation with nothingness as anything in modern American poetry" (*Robert Frost: Modern Poetic and the Landscapes of Self*), and William Doreski writes, "In many of Robert Frost's best poems the spirit of place that is New England is a diminishing thing, represented by a landscape in which the capacity for human renewal has apparently faded, leaving mad farm wives, eccentric telescopists, and most poignantly the ruins of hill farms abandoned as their owners die off or simply gave up trying to coax the recalcitrant and exhausted land into profit."

The truth seems to be that Frost's poems embody *both* the themes of human achievement and human failure, community and isolation, reasonableness and insanity. This poem is one of his darkest, though it is saved from total pessimism by the humanity of the census-taker's reaction to the desolation he finds. How much weight the reader puts upon that reaction rather depends upon how he/she reads the ambiguous final line.

Fire and Ice

Pre-reading

Ever *hated* someone or something passionately – I mean beyond reason.
Who or what? Why? With what result?
Ever *loved* someone or something passionately – I mean beyond reason.
Who or what? Why? With what result?

> Some say the world will end in fire;
> Some say in ice.
> From what I've tasted of desire
> I hold with those who favor fire.
> But if it had to perish twice,   5
> I think I know enough of hate
> To know that for destruction ice
> Is also great
> And would suffice.

Guiding Questions

1. Fire is associated by the speaker with the human emotion of desire and ice with hate. Why do you think that the speaker chooses the first as the more likely way for "the world" to end?
2. The last five lines of the poem involve humor and anti-climax. Give examples.
3. The poem is written in iambic tetrameter (four iambic feet in each line – except lines 2 and 8 and 9 which are dimeter, two iambic feet in each line). What kind of rhythm does this produce? How does that rhythm and tone affect your experience/understanding of the poem?

Final Thoughts

This is a poem very different from the New England pastorals for which Frost is known. It is a purely abstract meditation on man's self-destructive tendency. Reader's who miss the only semi-serious intent of the poem tend to misunderstand it.

The Earth will not last forever: either it will burn up or freeze. Human life is even more vulnerable: either global cooling or warming will eventually wipe us out even if the planet survives. Perhaps, however, humanity's destruction will come not from outside forces beyond our control but from within us. Some critics relate the poem to Dante's *The Inferno* and to the thought of the Greek philosopher Aristotle. It is not necessary to go there, however, to understand the poem's basic point: humans become self-destructive when they allow themselves to be guided by their passions (of either love or hate) uncontrolled by the operation of their reason. This is a poem which implicitly (but a little hopelessly) calls for balance.

Interpretations of the poem tend to miss the element of whimsy in the conclusion. There is a deliberate folksiness about the tone from the start with the repetition of "Some say..." as though the speaker is simply repeating gossip. There is humor in the nonsensical oxymoron "if it had to perish twice" since a thing *can* only perish once. Then, there is the anti-climax of the final two half-lines and of the final word "suffice" which seems mild and nuanced beside the extreme diction earlier in the poem ("end ... fire ... desire ... perish ... hate ... destruction").

Nothing Gold Can Stay

Pre-reading

What is the most perfect thing you ever saw in your life? How did you feel?
What happened to it?

Nature's first green is gold,
Her hardest hue to hold.
Her early leaf's a flower;
But only so an hour.
Then leaf subsides to leaf.   5
So Eden sank to grief,
So dawn goes down to day.
Nothing gold can stay.

Guiding Questions

1. The poem opens with apparent paradoxes: "green is gold" and "early
leaf's a flower." Try to explain what you think the speaker means in each
line. [Clue: Think of buds.]
2. What feeling about the change from flower to leaf is conveyed by the
word "subsides"?
3. Why did Eden sink to "grief"?
4. We normally think of dawn as coming up. In what sense can it be said to
go down?
5. The poem is in full rhyming couplets and each line ends in punctuation.
How does this contribute to its effect?
6. Alliteration occurs frequently. Comment on the effectiveness of its use.

7. Critic Bernetta Quinn concluded that this "is not a poem of sadness but of triumph." Do you agree? (quoted in Little 181).

Final Thoughts

Alfred R. Ferguson writes that "in fact the first flush of vegetation for the New England birch and the willow is not green but the haze of delicate gold" ("Frost and the Paradox of the Fortunate Fall"). If we accept this observation then, the paradox of the first line is only apparent; in reality, it is a statement of the literal truth of the first manifestation of spring. Similarly, the leaf, as it emerges from the bud, unfolds like a flower; for a moment it *is* a flower, but inevitably it evolves into its true state as leaf. In both changes there is an implicit sense of loss: gold has connotations of value and richness, and the flower has connotations of delicacy and beauty. Hence, there is a feeling of melancholy when green replaces gold and leaf replaces flower – a melancholy which is signified in the word "subsides" with its connotations of a decline.

The speaker links this idea from nature to theology by referencing the fall in the Garden of Eden from paradise to "grief" over the sinfulness of man. Then there is another paradox: "So dawn goes down to day." Normally we think of dawn as coming up as the sun rises over the horizon and climbs in the sky, but in fact the golden beauty of that sun fades as it rises, and the magical prospect of dawn evolves into the more prosaic day. Perfection is not possible; ideal situations cannot last forever.

Stopping by Woods on a Snowy Evening

Pre-reading

Ever had to choose between doing something that you wanted to do for yourself and doing something you felt yourself obliged to do for other people? (We all have. Like, you want to watch the game, but you have promised to visit someone who will certainly not be watching the game, so you have to choose.) Give a range of examples from the trivial to the serious. How did you resolve each conflict? How did you feel about the way you resolved these conflicts?

Suicide might be regarded as the most significant example of the conflict we have been talking about: the person who contemplates taking his/her own life normally has strong reasons for doing so, but what about their obligations to loved ones, friends and family?

Whose woods these are I think I know.
His house is in the village though;
He will not see me stopping here
To watch his woods fill up with snow.

My little horse must think it queer   5
To stop without a farmhouse near
Between the woods and frozen lake
The darkest evening of the year.

He gives his harness bells a shake
To ask if there is some mistake.   10
The only other sound's the sweep
Of easy wind and downy flake.

The woods are lovely, dark, and deep.
But I have promises to keep,
And miles to go before I sleep,   15
And miles to go before I sleep.

Guiding Questions

1. Again it is helpful to diagram or map the setting and dilemma of the poem adding quotations and comments.

2. What might the village represent (symbolize)? In what ways are the "woods" the antithesis of the "village"?

3. The horse shakes its head as if to question why the speaker has stopped. This is a perfectly realistic detail, but again it may be more than that. What aspect of the rider might the horse represent (symbolize)? (Clue: Look back to the reference to woods in "Into My Own.")

4. The speaker describes "the sweep / Of easy wind and downy flake." Is there anything ominous in this calm, beautiful description? (Clue: Think hypothermia!)

5. "The woods are lovely, dark, and deep." This is probably a very accurate description of the woods on this evening, but does it go beyond realism? What might the woods symbolize?

6. What kind of "promises" might the speaker have made? To whom?

7. The final line simply repeats the one before. Do you detect any difference in the tone of the two lines? Is the tone of the line regretful at the need to move on or optimistic about the life to which he is about to return? What impact does the last line have on your experience of and understanding of the poem?

8. In what senses might the poem be set on the "darkest evening of the year"?

9. The poem consists of four almost identically constructed stanzas (quatrains) rhyming: AABA BBCB CCDC DDDD. Note that in each stanza the word that ends the third line sets up the dominant rhyme of the following stanza with the exception of the final quatrain where all four lines have the same rhyme. Each line has four iambic feet. What contribution does the formal structure make to your experience of the poem?

Final Thoughts

Frost's friend W. H. Davies begins his poem "Leisure" with the lines, "WHAT is this life if, full of care, / We have no time to stand and stare?" This poem deals with the same issue: our lives are so full of 'stuff' to do that we just do not make the time to appreciate living in the moment. Had the term been around when Frost wrote, he might have called it 'mindfulness.' "*Mindfulness* is awareness that arises through paying attention, on purpose, in the present moment, non-judgementally" (Kabat-Zinn). That is what the speaker does in this poem despite the fact that a little voice inside tells him that he is being selfish and self-indulgent and that his first obligation must be to do what others rely on him to do.

The woods stand in opposition to the village. The contrast can be expressed in many ways: dark / light, solitude / community, nature / society, sensibility / reason, irrational / rational, selfishness / selflessness, etc. The woods might symbolize: death, suicide, the life of the imagination, writing poetry, etc. It is important to stress that the symbolism can just as well be positive as negative. One of the strengths of the poem is that the symbolism is suggestive not simply representative. The speaker is certainly tempted to respond to the call of the woods, but there are real dangers in doing so of which he hardly seems aware: the "sweep" of the "easy wind" might lull him to sleep and the "downy flake" might cover him like a soft blanket and he might freeze to death. For a moment, perhaps, the man might say with the poet Keats, "I have been half in love with easeful Death, / Call'd him soft names in many a mused rhyme" ("Ode to a Nightingale"), but in the end he decides to return to the world of duties and obligations, which is also the world where we actually get things done (like writing poetry and raising a family).

If there is a hint of wistful regret in the final two lines, there is also a clear sense of the speaker's determination to make the best use he can of his remaining life.

New Hampshire

The Need of Being Versed in Country Things

Pre-reading

What life-lessons do you think are taught by living in the city (being what we might call 'city-smart')? What life-lessons do you think are taught by living in the country (being what we might call "Versed in Country Things.")

The house had gone to bring again
To the midnight sky a sunset glow.
Now the chimney was all of the house that stood.
Like a pistil after the petals go.

The barn opposed across the way,   5
That would have joined the house in flame
Had it been the will of the wind, was left
To bear forsaken the place's name.

No more it opened with all one end
For teams that came by the stony road   10
To drum on the floor with scurrying hoofs
And brush the mow with the summer load.

The birds that came to it through the air
At broken windows flew out and in,
Their murmur more like the sigh we sigh   15
From too much dwelling on what has been.

Yet for them the lilac renewed its leaf,
And the aged elm, though touched with fire;
And the dry pump flung up an awkward arm;
And the fence post carried a strand of wire.   20

For them there was really nothing sad.
But though they rejoiced in the nest they kept,
One had to be versed in country things
Not to believe the phoebes wept.

118

Study Guide

Guiding Questions

The poem is written in six quatrains rhymed ABCB.

1. The setting is, as in "The Census-Taker," an isolated farmhouse. The key differences are that this house burned down and that there is even less evidence of the lives of the people who lived there. Explain exactly how the house brought "again / To the midnight sky a sunset glow."

2. The pistil is the female reproductive part of a flower, the part sticking up in the middle of the blossom that is pollinated by bees. Is there more to the simile of chimney / pistil than just physical resemblance?

3. How does the personification of the wind in the second quatrain convey the speaker's sense of a close connection between the human world and the world of nature?

4. Although it is still standing, the barn no longer performs its function in relation to the farm. What specific example is given in stanza three?

5. In stanza four, the speaker personifies the sound of the birds flying in and out of the ruined house. What very human emotion do the birds seem to him to be exhibiting?

6. The relationship of the birds with the ruined house is, however, different from its relationship with humans. The speaker mentions four ways (one in each line of stanza five) in which they still inhabit the ruin. What are they? Notice the speaker's use of the active voice: the lilac and elm "renewed," the pump "flung up," and the fence "carried." What is important about the choice of verbs here?

Note: In the final line "phoebes" are a colloquial name for the American tyrant flycatcher (Tyrannidae), a family of birds with over four hundred species.

7. In what way does the speaker change everything that he has earlier said about the birds feeling the sadness of this abandoned house? What does being "versed in country things" teach humans about their relationship with the fauna and flora of nature? Is this presented as an optimistic or a pessimistic conclusion?

Final Thoughts

"Anthropomorphism is the attribution of human traits, emotions, or intentions to non-human entities. It is considered to be an innate tendency of human psychology" (Wikipedia contributors. "Anthropomorphism"). "The Need of Being Versed in Country Things" is a corrective to the human tendency toward anthropomorphism. At first the speaker seeks to impose human concerns onto all aspects of the natural world. His means of doing this is personification: the house seems to have burned down at midnight intentionally "to bring again" the sunset of a few hours previously; the chimney stands like a pistil seeming to offer the prospect of rebirth; the "will of the wind" seems to have saved the barn to preserve "the place's name"; and the birds seem to "sigh" as humans do at the sadness of "what has been."

At the start of stanza five, the speaker abandons his romantic notion of the interdependence of the human and natural realms; such ideas are nonsense as anyone versed in country things knows very well. The birds live in the moment. To them, the ruin is as functional as the house ever was. Only the human mind is capable of thinking back in time and comparing present with past. The flora and fauna are incapable of recalling a past and of mourning the fact that it can never return. The human alone has to face the implications of the fact that the ruined house was utterly and irrevocably destroyed by fire; unlike the elm, it will not regenerate, and unlike the birds, the people will never return. This is the harsh reality and lesson of nature. "Those not versed in country things think that nature cares about human beings and other living things. Those who are versed know about the indifference of nature, that it does not respond to human affairs" (Fagan 232). There is nothing sad about the burning down of a house – it happens.

Appendix 1: Swinging on a Birch Tree by Lucy Larcom (1824-1893)

SWINGING on a birch-tree
To a sleepy tune,
Hummed by all the breezes
In the month of June!
Little leaves a-flutter
Sound like dancing drops
Of a brook on pebbles, –
Song that never stops.

Up and down we seesaw:
Up into the sky;
How it opens on us,
Like a wide blue eye!
You and I are sailors
Rocking on a mast;
And the world's our vessel:
Ho! she sails so fast!

Blue, blue sea around us;
Not a ship in sight;
They will hang out lanterns
When they pass, to-night.
We with ours will follow
Through the midnight deep;
Not a thought of danger,
Though the crew's asleep.

O, how still the air is!
There an oriole flew;
What a jolly whistle!
He's a sailor, too.
Yonder is his hammock
In the elm-top high:
One more ballad, messmate!
Sing it as you fly!

Up and down we seesaw;
Down into the grass,
Scented fern, and rosebuds,
All a woven mass.
That's the sort of carpet
Fitted for our feet;
Tapestry nor velvet
Is so rich and neat.

Swinging on a birch-tree!
This is summer joy,
Fun for all vacation,—
Don't you think so, boy?
Up and down to seesaw,
Merry and at ease,
Careless as a brook is,
Idle as the breeze.

Appendix 2: Reading Group Use of the Study Guide Questions

Although there are both closed and open questions in the Study Guide, very few of them have simple, right or wrong answers. They are designed to encourage in-depth discussion, disagreement, and (eventually) consensus. Above all, they aim to encourage readers to go to the text to support their conclusions and interpretations.

I am not so arrogant as to presume to tell readers how they should use this resource. I used it in the following ways, each of which ensured that group members were well prepared for group discussion and presentations.

1. Set a reading assignment for the group and tell everyone to be aware that the questions will be the focus of whole group discussion at the next meeting.

2. Set a reading assignment for the group and allocate particular questions to sections of the group (e.g. if there are four questions, divide the group into four sections, etc.).
In the meeting, form discussion groups containing one person who has prepared each question and allow time for feedback within the groups.
Have feedback to the whole the on each question by picking a group at random to present their answers and to follow up with a group discussion.

3. Set a reading assignment for the group, but do not allocate questions.
In the meeting, divide readers into groups and allocate to each group one of the questions related to the reading assignment, the answer to which they will have to present formally to the meeting.
Allow time for discussion and preparation.

4. Set a reading assignment for the group, but do not allocate questions.
In the meeting, divide readers into groups and allocate to each group one of the questions related to the reading assignment.
Allow time for discussion and preparation.
Now reconfigure the groups so that each group contains at least one person who has prepared each question and allow time for feedback within the groups.

5. Before starting to read the text, allocate specific questions to individuals or pairs. (It is best not to allocate all questions to allow for other approaches and variety. One in three questions or one in four seems about right.) Tell readers that they will be leading the group discussion on their question. They will need to start with a brief presentation of the issues and then conduct a question and answer session. After this, they will be expected to present a brief review of the discussion.

6. Having finished the text, arrange the meeting into groups of 3, 4 or 5. Tell each group to select as many questions from the Study Guide as there are members of the group.

Each individual is responsible for drafting out an answer to one question, and each answer should be substantial.

Each group as a whole is then responsible for discussing, editing and suggesting improvements to each answer.

Appendix 3: Literary Terms

Poetic Terms

Alliteration: when a number of words close together begin with the same first consonant sound (e.g., "Round the rugged rock...") – to understand the contribution of alliteration ask yourself: short or long sounds; soft or harsh sounds; how is the sound of the vowels appropriate to what the words mean?

Assonance: when two or more words repeat the same vowel sound but with different consonant sounds (e.g., "down to the slow, black, sloe-black, crow-black fishing-boat-bobbing sea") – to understand the contribution of assonance ask yourself: short or long sounds; soft or harsh sounds; how is the sound of the vowels appropriate to what the words mean? [Note that, as in the examples above, alliteration and assonance can work together.]

Blank verse: Non-rhyming verse written in iambic pentameter (i.e., each line has ten syllables arranged in pairs: unstressed / stressed).

Caesura: when a break or pause occurs in the middle of a line of verse – the break may be indicated by a punctuation mark or it may be a natural pause.

Couplet: the name for two lines of poetry – they may be rhymed or unrhymed.

Enjambment: when a line of poetry does not end with a pause but 'runs-on' to the next line without a syntactical or rhythmical break – its opposite is an end stopped line which ends with terminal punctuation at the end of a sentence or clause.

Foot / Feet: lines of poetry are divided into units called feet – each foot normally has two syllables and most often these are iambic (unstressed / stressed), but there are other arrangements – it is the pattern of feet that establishes the meter of a poem.

Meter: the pattern of stressed and unstressed syllables in a line or lines of poetry – meter gives poetry its rhythmic pattern.

Iambic meter: an unstressed syllable followed by a stressed syllable – English is by its nature an iambic language. (There are other meters.)

Onomatopoeia: when the pronunciation of a word actually mimics the sound of the object or action it describes (e.g., buzz, sizzling, yapping).

Rhyme scheme: the repeated pattern of rhyme that comes at the end of lines of poetry – full rhyme is when the stressed vowels and consonants sound identical (e.g., chain, brain) – half rhyme is when the stressed consonants match but the vowel sounds do not (e.g., long, swing).

Stanza / verse: four or more lines with the same length, meter, and rhyme scheme – like paragraphs in prose, stanzas are composed of connected thoughts separated from other stanzas by a space.

General Terms

Ambiguous, ambiguity: when a statement is unclear in meaning – ambiguity may be deliberate or accidental.

Analogy: a comparison which treats two things as identical in one or more specified ways.

Antagonist: a character or force opposing the protagonist.

Antithesis: the complete opposite of something.

Climax: the conflict to which the action has been building since the start of the play or story.

Colloquialism: the casual, informal mainly spoken language of ordinary people – often called "slang."

Connotation: the ideas, feelings and associations generated by a word or phrase.

Dark comedy: comedy which has a serious implication – comedy that deals with subjects not usually treated humorously (e.g., death).

Dialogue: a conversation between two or more people in direct speech.

Diction: the writer's choice of words in order to create a particular effect.

Equivocation: saying something which is capable of two interpretations with the intention of misrepresenting the truth.

Euphemism: a polite word for an ugly truth – for example, a person is said to be sleeping when they are actually dead.

Fallacy: a misconception resulting from incorrect reasoning.

First person: first person singular is "I" and plural is "we".

Foreshadowing: a statement or action which gives the reader a hint of what is likely to happen later in the narrative.

Genre: the type of literature into which a particular text falls (e.g. drama, poetry, novel).

Image, imagery: figurative language such as simile, metaphor, personification etc., or a description which conjures up a particularly vivid picture.

Imply, implication: when the text suggests to the reader a meaning which it does not actually state.

Infer, inference: the reader's act of going beyond what is stated in the text to draw conclusions.

Irony, ironic: a form of humor which undercuts the apparent meaning of a statement:

Conscious irony: irony used deliberately by a writer or character;

Unconscious irony: a statement or action which has significance for the reader of which the character is unaware;

Dramatic irony: when an action has an important significance that is obvious to the reader but not to one or more of the characters;

Tragic irony: when a character says (or does) something which will have a serious, even fatal, consequence for him/ her. The audience is aware of the error, but the character is not;

Verbal irony: the conscious use of particular words which are appropriate to what is being said.

Juxtaposition: literally putting two things side by side for purposes of comparison and/ or contrast.

Literal: the surface level of meaning that a statement has.

Melodramatic: action and/or dialogue that is inflated or extravagant – frequently used for comic effect.

Metaphor, metaphorical: the description of one thing by direct comparison with another (e.g. the coal-black night). Extended metaphor: a comparison which is developed at length.

Mood: the feelings and emotions contained in and/ or produced by a work of art (text, painting, music, etc.).

Motif: a frequently repeated idea, image or situation in a text.

Motivation: why a character acts as he/she does – in modern literature motivation is seen as psychological.

Narrator: the voice that the reader hears in the text – not to be confused with the author.

Oxymoron: the juxtaposition of two terms normally thought of as opposite (e.g. the silent scream).

Paradox, paradoxical: a statement or situation which appears self-contradictory and therefore absurd.

Pathos: is pity, or rather the ability of a text to make the audience or reader feel pity.

Perspective: point of view from which a story, or an incident within a story, is told.

Personified, personification: a simile or metaphor in which an inanimate object or abstract idea is described by comparison with a human.

Plot: a chain of events linked by cause and effect.

Protagonist: the character who initiates the action and is most likely to have the sympathy of the audience.

Realism: a text that describes the action in a way that appears to reflect life.

Sarcasm: stronger than irony – it involves a deliberate attack on a person or idea with the intention of mocking.

Setting: the environment in which the narrative (or part of the narrative) takes place.

Simile: a description of one thing by explicit comparison with another (e.g. my love is like a red, red rose). Extended simile: a comparison which is developed at length.

Style: the way in which a writer chooses to express him/ herself. Style is a vital aspect of meaning since how something is expressed can crucially affect what is being written or spoken.

Symbol, symbolic, symbolism, symbolize: a physical object which comes to represent an abstract idea (e.g. the sun may symbolize life).

Themes: important concepts, beliefs and ideas explored and presented in a text.

Third person: third person singular is "he/ she/ it" and plural is "they" – authors often write novels in the third person.

Tone: literally the sound of a text – How words sound (either in the mouth of an actor or the head of a reader) can crucially affect meaning.

Bibliography

Bloom, Harold, editor. *Modern Critical Views: Robert Frost*. New York: Chelsea House, 1986. Print.

Course Hero. "The Poems of Robert Frost Study Guide." *Course Hero.* 10 Nov. 2017. Web. 21 June 2019.

Cox, James, editor. Twentieth Century Views: Robert Frost. Englewood Cliffs: Prentice-Hall, 1962. Print.

Doreski, William. "Robert Frost's 'The Census Taker' and the Problem of Wilderness". *Twentieth Century Literature*, Volume 34, Number 1 (Spring 1988), Hofstrat University. 17 Dec. 2014. Web. 20 Jun. 2019.

Fagan, Deirdre. *Critical Companion to Robert Frost*. New York: Infobase, 2007. Print.

Kendal, Tim. *The Art of Robert Frost*. New Haven: Yale, 2012. Print.

Little, Michael. *Bloom's How to Write about Robert Frost*. New York: Infobase, 2010. Print.

Spacey, Andrew. *Owlcation.* 10 Nov. 2017. Web. 21 June 2019.

SparkNotes Editors. "SparkNote on Frost's Early Poems." SparkNotes.com. SparkNotes LLC. 2002. Web. 20 Jun. 2019.

Squires, Radcliffe. *The Major Themes of Robert Frost*. Ann Arbor: University of Michigan Press, 1963. Print.

The Reverend Lyle Thorne Mysteries

If you enjoy detective short stories, you will love my series featuring policeman turned vicar Lyle Thorne (1860-1947)

Investigations of The Reverend Lyle Thorne (Volume One)

Thorne investigates five cases spanning the years 1911-1927:

The fallen woman loses more than her life...

The anonymous cleric pleads for a murder suspect...

The Italian bride is frightened by mysterious disappearances...

The missing betrothed vanishes the day before her wedding...

A hanged man is still swinging in a locked room...

Further Investigations of The Reverend Lyle Thorne (Volume Two)

Thorne investigates five cases spanning the years 1910-1912:

The wedding of an American heiress and divorcee is cancelled by the inexplicable disappearance of her ring...

An Oxford antiquarian is found lying on a hoard of medieval coins...

The young bride-to-be of a rich widower receives frightening threats...

A Sussex landowner walks calmly into the courtyard of his house and vanishes...

Thorne must find a husband who has taken great care not to be found...

Early Investigations of Lyle Thorne (Volume Three)

Thorne investigates five cases spanning the years 1876 to 1889:

In Thorne's first ever investigation, his father is accused of murder by a dead man...

Having been told to meet his step-father at 1 p.m., a young boy sets off from home at 12.45 p.m. and is never seen alive again...

Twins plan and execute a perfect murder...

A baby disappears from the nursery of the London home of the Duke and Duchess of Albermarle...

Thorne's investigations put a name to Jack the Ripper but at terrible personal cost...

Sanditon Investigations of The Rev. Lyle Thorne (Volume Four)

Thorne investigates five cases spanning the years 1912-1914:

A young girl disappears for the second time, this time from an enclosed garden...

A modern painter dies of a heart attack – a natural death until the coffin falls and breaks open at the burial...

A bishop in line to become Archbishop of Canterbury is poisoned in his own library...

Thorne's curate encounters a young girl abandoned on the promenade...

The discovery of the body of a man stabbed to death more than two centuries ago sets Thorne the ultimate investigative challenge...

Final Investigations of The Rev. Lyle Thorne (Volume Five)

Thorne investigates five cases spanning the years 1927-1948:

A photographer's kiosk is burned down on the same day as Sanditon's biggest jewel robbery...

A school master is found poisoned a few days before his retirement...

A shell-shocked soldier becomes obsessed by "the lady in the dark"...

A young railway worker implicated in a robbery is found murdered...

Thorne witnesses the discovery of an 'impossible' murder-robbery at a bank in Sanditon...

Lost Investigation of The Rev. Lyle Thorne (Volume Six)

Thorne investigates five cases spanning the years 1908 - 1912:

A runner is seen entering the tunnel under a railway line and is never seen again...

Rev. Thorne's curate is accused of the theft of a valuable sapphire pendant from a dying woman...

The body of a local man is washed up on Sanditon beach, but his empty cottage is found to be locked from the inside...

The abrupt dismissal of a scullery maid alerts Thorne to two crimes...

A mysterious and glamorous American widow is abducted, and the body of her abductor is found the next day...

Official Investigations of Lyle Thorne (Volume Seven)

As a young member of the Metropolitan Police, Thorne investigates five cases spanning the years 1881 – 1887:

An apparently simple case of murder reveals Thorne's ability to see beyond the obvious...

Three young women plan a holiday excursion to Margate, but events take a tragic turn...

Thorne realizes that an innocent man will be hung and that it is his evidence that has convicted him...

A weekly tea party leaves one woman dead and another in the hospital...

An international criminal bets the Commissioner of Police that he can commit the perfect crime...

Clerical Investigations of The Rev. Lyle Thorne (Volume Eight)

As a newly ordained minister in the Church of England, Thorne investigates three cases spanning the years 1896 – 1898:

A curate inexplicably leaves his parish in the middle of the night, just as two years earlier the former vicar had also left...

A vicar in Leeds is found kneeling over the dead body of his wife with the murder weapon in his hand...

The manuscript of an ancient Lindisfarne gospel and its modern translation disappear from a locked strongbox, in a locked desk, in a locked room...

About the Author

Ray Moore was born in Nottingham, England. He obtained his Master's Degree in Literature from Lancaster University and taught in secondary education for twenty-eight years before relocating to Florida with his wife. There he taught English and Information Technology in the International Baccalaureate Program. He is now a full-time writer and fitness fanatic and leads a reading group at a local library.

Website: http://www.raymooreauthor.com

Ray strives to make his texts the best that they can be. If you have any comments or question about this book *please* contact the author through his email: **villageswriter@gmail.com**

Also by Ray Moore:

Books are available from amazon.com and from barnesandnoble.com as paperbacks and some from online eBook retailers.

Fiction:

1066: Year of the Five Kings is a novel of the most consequential year in the history of England.

The Lyle Thorne Mysteries Volumes One to Eight. (as detailed previously)

Non-fiction:

The *Critical Introduction series* is written for high school teachers and students and for college undergraduates. Each volume gives an in-depth analysis of a key text:

"The Stranger" by Albert Camus: A Critical Introduction (Revised Second Edition)

"The General Prologue" by Geoffrey Chaucer: A Critical Introduction

"Pride and Prejudice" by Jane Austen: A Critical Introduction

"The Great Gatsby" by F. Scott Fitzgerald: A Critical Introduction

The *Text and Critical Introduction series* differs from the Critical introduction series as these books contain the original text and in the case of the medieval texts an interlinear translation to aid the understanding of the text. The commentary allows the reader to develop a deeper understanding of the text and themes within the text.

"Sir Gawain and the Green Knight": Text and Critical Introduction*

"The General Prologue" by Geoffrey Chaucer: Text and Critical Introduction*

"Heart of Darkness" by Joseph Conrad: Text and Critical Introduction*

*"Henry V" by William Shakespeare: Text and Critical Introduction**
*"Oedipus Rex" by Sophocles: Text and Critical Introduction**
*"A Room with a View" By E.M. Forster: Text and Critical Introduction**
"The Sign of Four" by Sir Arthur Conan Doyle Text and Critical Introduction
*"The Wife of Bath's Prologue and Tale" by Geoffrey Chaucer: Text and Critical Introduction**
Jane Austen: The Complete Juvenilia: Text and Critical Introduction

Study Guides - listed alphabetically by author
Study Guides offer an in-depth look at aspects of a text. They generally include an introduction to the characters, genre, themes, setting, tone of a text. They also may include activities on helpful literary terms as well as graphic organizers to aid understanding of the plot and different perspectives of characters.

*   * denotes also available as an eBook*
"ME and EARL and the Dying GIRL" by Jesse Andrews: A Study Guide
*Study Guide to "Alias Grace" by Margaret Atwood**
*Study Guide to "The Handmaid's Tale" by Margaret Atwood**
"Pride and Prejudice" by Jane Austen: A Study Guide
"Moloka'i" by Alan Brennert: A Study Guide
*"Wuthering Heights" by Emily Brontë: A Study Guide **
*Study Guide on "Jane Eyre" by Charlotte Brontë**
"The Myth of Sisyphus" by Albert Camus: A Study Guide
"The Stranger" by Albert Camus: A Study Guide
*"The Myth of Sisyphus" and "The Stranger" by Albert Camus: Two Study Guides **
Study Guide to "Death Comes to the Archbishop" by Willa Cather
"The Awakening" by Kate Chopin: A Study Guide
Study Guide to Seven Short Stories by Kate Chopin
Study Guide to "Ready Player One" by Ernest Cline
Study Guide to "Disgrace" by J. M. Coetzee
"The Meursault Investigation" by Kamel Daoud: A Study Guide
*Study Guide on "Great Expectations" by Charles Dickens**
*"The Sign of Four" by Sir Arthur Conan Doyle: A Study Guide **
Study Guide to "Manhattan Beach" by Jennifer Egan
"The Wasteland, Prufrock and Poems" by T.S. Eliot: A Study Guide
*Study Guide on "Birdsong" by Sebastian Faulks**
"The Great Gatsby" by F. Scott Fitzgerald: A Study Guide

134

"A Room with a View" by E. M. Forster: A Study Guide
"Looking for Alaska" by John Green: A Study Guide
"Paper Towns" by John Green: A Study Guide
Study Guide to "Turtles All the Way Down" by John Green
Study Guide to "Florida" by Lauren Groff
Study Guide on "Catch-22" by Joseph Heller *
"Unbroken" by Laura Hillenbrand: A Study Guide
"The Kite Runner" by Khaled Hosseini: A Study Guide
"A Thousand Splendid Suns" by Khaled Hosseini: A Study Guide
"The Secret Life of Bees" by Sue Monk Kidd: A Study Guide
Study Guide on "The Invention of Wings" by Sue Monk Kidd
Study Guide to "Fear and Trembling" by Søren Kierkegaard
"Go Set a Watchman" by Harper Lee: A Study Guide
Study Guide to "Pachinko" by Min Jin Lee
"On the Road" by Jack Kerouac: A Study Guide
Study Guide on "Life of Pi" by Yann Martel*
Study Guide to "Death of a Salesman" by Arthur Miller
Study Guide to "The Bluest Eye" by Toni Morrison
Study Guide to "Reading Lolita in Tehran" by Azir Nafisi
Study Guide to "The Sympathizer" by Viet Thanh Nguyen
"Animal Farm" by George Orwell: A Study Guide
Study Guide on "Nineteen Eighty-Four" by George Orwell
Study Guide to "The Essex Serpent" by Sarah Perry
Study Guide to "Selected Poems" and Additional Poems by Sylvia Plath*
"An Inspector Calls" by J.B. Priestley: A Study Guide
Study Guide to "Cross Creek" by Marjorie Kinnan Rawlings
"Esperanza Rising" by Pam Munoz Ryan: A Study Guide
Study Guide to "The Catcher in the Rye" by J.D. Salinger
"Where'd You Go, Bernadette" by Maria Semple: A Study Guide
"Henry V" by William Shakespeare: A Study Guide
Study Guide on "Macbeth" by William Shakespeare *
"Othello" by William Shakespeare: A Study Guide *
Study Guide on "Antigone" by Sophocles*
"Oedipus Rex" by Sophocles: A Study Guide
"Cannery Row" by John Steinbeck: A Study Guide
"East of Eden" by John Steinbeck: A Study Guide
"The Grapes of Wrath" by John Steinbeck: A Study Guide
"Of Mice and Men" by John Steinbeck: A Study Guide*

"The Goldfinch" by Donna Tartt: A Study Guide
Study Guide to "The Hate U Give" by Angie Thomas
"Walden; or, Life in the Woods" by Henry David Thoreau: A Study Guide
Study Guide to "Cat's Cradle" by Kurt Vonnegut
"The Bridge of San Luis Rey" by Thornton Wilder: A Study Guide *
Study Guide on "The Book Thief" by Markus Zusak

Study Guides available *only* as e-books:

Study Guide on "Cross Creek" by Marjorie Kinnan Rawlings.
Study Guide on "Heart of Darkness" by Joseph Conrad:
Study Guide on "The Mill on the Floss" by George Eliot
Study Guide on "Lord of the Flies" by William Golding
Study Guide on "Nineteen Eighty-Four" by George Orwell
Study Guide on "Henry IV Part 2" by William Shakespeare
Study Guide on "Julius Caesar" by William Shakespeare
Study Guide on "The Pearl" by John Steinbeck
Study Guide on "Slaughterhouse-Five" by Kurt Vonnegut

New titles are added regularly.

Readers' Guides

Readers' Guides offer an introduction to important aspects of the text and questions for personal reflection and/or discussion. Guides are written for individual readers who wish to explore texts in depth and for members of Reading Circles who wish to make their discussions of texts more productive.

A Reader's Guide to Becoming by Michelle Obama
A Reader's Guide to Educated: A Memoir by Tara Westover

Teacher resources: Ray also publishes many more study guides and other resources for classroom use on the 'Teachers Pay Teachers' website: **http://www.teacherspayteachers.com/Store/Raymond-Moore**

Printed in Great Britain
by Amazon